Betjeman COUNTRY

Betjeman COUNTRY

FRANK DELANEY

Photographs by James Ravilious

Drawings by Leonora Ison

HODDER AND STOUGHTON

JOHN MURRAY

By the same author
JAMES JOYCE'S ODYSSEY

British Library Cataloguing in Publication Data

Delaney, Frank
  Betjeman Country
  1. Betjeman, John – Homes and haunts
  I.Title
  821'.912   PR6003. E77

  ISBN 0 340 34151 3 (Hodder and Stoughton)
  ISBN 0 7195 4086 0 (John Murray)

Text copyright © 1983 by Frank Delaney.
New photographs copyright © James Ravilious.
Line drawings copyright © Leonora Ison.
First printed 1983.
Second impression 1984.
All rights reserved.

Printed in Great Britain for Hodder and Stoughton Limited,
Mill Road, Dunton Green, Sevenoaks, Kent and John Murray
(Publishers) Ltd, 50 Albemarle Street, London W1X 4BD, by
BAS Printers Ltd, Over Wallop, Hampshire.

Hodder and Stoughton Editorial Office:
47 Bedford Square, London WC1B 3DP.

BOOK DESIGN BY SHARYN TROUGHTON

CONTENTS

INTRODUCTION

This is a travel book, the notes of quiet visits to random places all with one thing in common – they are connected with the poems of Sir John Betjeman. The idea sprang at first from the sheer enjoyment of his verses, so wistful and comic and thoughtful and accessible and immensely quotable, as full of recognisable personality and incident as a daily newspaper. He is a reporter-poet, a suburban remembrancer, a broadcaster-poet, whose images are never so finely tuned that you require special antennae to receive them and he is now the most popular living poet in the English language.

But a *travel* book? The stimulus grew following a BBC radio programme when he said, "I'm inspired by a place and then I work round it. It starts as an inspiration and ends as a cross-word which has to be worked out." Others, who delve more deeply, more critically, have even formed the opinion that the sense of place is fundamental to his poems. Introducing a Betjeman collection published in 1945, John Sparrow, later Warden of All Souls College, Oxford, wrote:

> He is the painter of the particular, the recognisable land-scape; his trees are not merely real trees with their roots in the earth, they are conifers with their roots in the red sand of Camberley, feathery ash in leathery Lambourne, or forsythia in the Banbury Road.

Could a traveller in Britain, then, use John Betjeman as a guide? Read the *Collected Poems*, or the autobiography *Summoned by Bells,* and you may steer by his landmarks – Cornwall's lanes and beaches, Oxford's colleges and lawns, Marl-borough and the Wiltshire Downs, churches in the City of London.

But since the traveller must also observe the natives, is mere sense of place not insufficient? Setting a poet to catch a poet, a review by Philip Larkin satisfied that point.

> His subjects are children's parties, handsome tennis-girls, the arrest of Oscar Wilde and church furnishing, mingled with snatches of autobiography and personal statements about death and lust and remorse, with the occasional flight into force or fantasy. What makes them perplexing is their ambivalence (both funny and serious): what makes them memorable is the utter sincerity of their feeling and the precise vivacity of their language.

7

But traveller – beware! The first difficulty lay in the fact that he has always been so prolific. Apart from the poems – many, if not most, of which contain some topographical reference – reams of newsprint accrued from his weekly "Men and Buildings" series which he wrote for years in the *Daily Telegraph*. Add innumerable introductions, prefaces, commentaries, a book or two, a variety of county guides, the comprehensive *Guide to Parish Churches of England and Wales*, and the entire collection of his works, if put together as a volume, would amount to a social history of Britain in the twentieth century, albeit with eccentricities of emphasis – architecture, churches, railway trains, snobbery. But it finally seemed sensible, despite the seduction of that huge body of material, to pursue the original intention and seek out that curious land which might be called "Betjeman country".

As far as I was concerned John Betjeman had already established his credentials. His poems about Ireland were perceptive, sympathetic, gentle and completely lacking in any infuriating patronisation: few, if any, English poets had perceived Ireland in such an enthusiastic and understanding fashion, and the places that he wrote about were identifiable. Therefore Betjeman writing on his own home ground could even be educational.

Travelling through Britain might offer opportunities for anthropological, cultural and social discovery – provided the tongue was never too far from the cheek. Was it true that there was an England in there, that *Mrs Dale's Diary* and *The Lady* were not fiction? On the evidence in the verses, Betjeman country is a warm and comforting territory of seaside golf clubs, cottage hospitals, tennis courts, privet hedges, belfries, wrought-iron railings and lilac trees in the crescent, chintz tea-shops, and churches, silent squares, billiard-rooms and branch lines. A thousand years from now excavations will yield Coronation mugs, tea and cocoa tins labelled Mazzawattee and Epps, bottles marked Drene and Innoxa, fragments of stained glass. And the natives, the inhabitants, of this toyland – who are they? Likeable but impossible colonels' wives, big, gentle tennis-playing girls, meticulous golf club secretaries, doctors, dons, dessicated parsons, civil servants and church mice, snobs, pony-tailed pony-club members, secretaries, executives, architects. No reason, then, why a series of journeys into Betjeman country might not be as rewarding as a trip up the Orinoco – and a great deal less hazardous.

*   *   *

"On the backs of cigarette packets and old letters [Betjeman has written] I write down my lines, crossing out and changing.

When I reach home I transfer the whole to foolscap and cross out and change again. Then I start reciting the lines aloud, either driving a car or on solitary walks, until the sound of the words satisfies me." Betjeman has never claimed to belong to any ethereal band of frail, silvered thinkers whose lines request analysis rather than enjoyment. In the same apologia – he has always felt the need to be defensive of his efforts – he wrote, "As early as I can remember I have read and written verse. I have always preferred it to prose, known that its composition was my vocation and anything else I have written in my life has been primarily a means of earning money in order to buy the free time in which to write poetry."

He began to write at school, early poems for Marlborough's magazines – official and alternative. The first appearance between the covers of a book came at the age of nineteen, in 1925, in an anthology, *Public School Verse*; his first professional poem, "Death in Leamington", was accepted by the *London Mercury* and included in his first collection, *Mount Zion*, which was published by his friend Edward James in 1931 – when Betjeman was only 25. From 1931 poems, articles, short essays, dissertations, broadcasts poured out up to 1974 when the last collection over which he presided, *A Nip in the Air*, appeared (a subsequent volume, *Uncollected Poems*, was compiled from forgotten pieces discovered in a Canadian archive). A knighthood in 1969, and the Laureateship in 1972 institutionalised the poet and his image. His television audiences saw an amused, charming and dear poet, with a quirky curiosity and eccentric enthusiasms for old churches, their musty incumbents, for Victorian railway carriages and Gothicry. He even had his own childhood teddy bear called Archibald which misled *The Times* to call a profile "By Appointment: Teddy Bear To The Nation."

But there were dissemblings at work. Philip Larkin saw through them, wrote about the "irrepressible fun . . . native to Betjeman, the wooden horse with which he penetrated the Left-Book-Club thirties and the angst-ridden forties so that his subversive aesthetic could slowly possess us." And in character, John Betjeman is not entirely the chuckling, amused and amusing, cheerful, eager-to-please individual which the larger public perceives. Between the lines of his poems lies a deeply melancholic man, long preoccupied with age and death and decay, a fearful spirit whose perceptions move far beyond the simple. His passions have always run deep, as have his guilts and worries; and in the apparent simplicity of his form and content, he has either been deliberately deceptive or misperceived.

In recent years illness has reduced his capacity to write and his memory is not what he would wish it to be. He sits, quiet and still, in a front, ground-floor room of a small house in Chelsea, pullover, striped shirt. Answers are thoughtful but pertinent and pert: "Yes, I remember her – she was the sort of girl who had boyfriends called 'Boris'." He still laughs often, infectiously and gleefully, asks visitors to read to him, never his own lines. If the poem is moving, tears fill his eyes.

His mail is enormous, much of it from correspondents with poetic ambitions. The good ones receive encouragement, the bad ones tact and he professes astonishment at his own popularity.

He has always responded violently to adverse criticism. "My verses are my children, sometimes too private to be shown in public. They are part of me and attacks on them I take as personal and feel inclined to answer in terms of personal abuse. When they are published my verses are generally grown up into comparative strangers." His most vociferous critics have called him a versifier, a rhymester, a minor poet who scribbles light verse, never to be taken seriously. But those who defend him are equally vocal in their praise. Philip Larkin wrote:

> Betjeman has long been accepted as a writer of original and amusing light verse who is able at times to touch deeper emotions, but the description hardly does justice to the range of his poetry, that takes in uproarious comedy, delicate pathos and brutal honesty with an equally sure touch. (He has) . . . simply created the taste by which he is relished.

In prose, Sir John Betjeman's output has been mainly journalistic, columns, essays, long radio talks. As a film critic for Beaverbrook he produced no memorable insights (apart from the well-known, oft-repeated and not at all apocryphal story that he bawdily persuaded Myrna Loy to let him write that she was interested in architecture, "English Perpendicular"). His writings on buildings, though, were deeply-researched and passionately expressed. His architectural knowledge climbs towards encyclopaedic levels, even if, in more than one instance, he has revised his opinions entirely. His affections have always been directed towards structures and systems which retain old values and virtues. The combination of poetry, architecture, churchiness and observation of the middle classes gives Betjeman a wholly individual flavour.

He points out the poets whom he has admired – with Tennyson in the forefront – and identifies with a host of forgotten Victorian and Edwardian poets, Crabbe, Thomas Hood, William Barnes, whose metres he borrows. He has always sought simplicity and accessibility, never claimed to belong to the world of high literary technology: "I love suburbs and gaslights and Pont Street and Gothic Revival churches and mineral railways, provincial towns and Garden cities", as if he feared damage or pomposity or pretentiousness by being taken too seriously.

*   *   *

No one word can characterise a travel brochure of Betjeman country. His early volume *Continual Dew* (thirty-three poems, originally printed, with comic inconsequence, on firework paper) was sub-titled "A Little Book of Bourgeois Verse". Thus misled, one left-wing critic condemned the poems as "full of the prejudices of the nineteenth-century bourgeoisie in their most corrupt and inverted forms". But is it not bourgeois to have a horror of the bourgeois? And bourgeois or not Sir John Betjeman's poems take the traveller by the hand, to childhood haunts and adult fears, to places of worship and ideal love. To travel through Betjeman country choose favourite poems, keep an eye on the prose, look up at the buildings and he becomes an illuminating and rewarding guide. North London, Marlborough, Oxford, Ireland, Berkshire, Bath, Metro-Land – Betjeman country is a jigsaw in verse, with some pieces missing. He did, for example, have an obsession with the Isle of Man, but only touches on it in his poems; and if East Anglia captured his heart a long time ago – why the landscapes and churches only, why not the people? And no body of poems relating to the far North, or Scotland? But an exhaustive analysis of his topography is a different matter, one in which the burden of detail might take precedence over the enthusiasm.

*   *   *

Travel ought to have illustrations: in this book they come from four sources. First, I have quoted from Sir John Betjeman's own works in poetry and prose, and such quotation presented problems of selectivity. Wherever possible I have avoided quoting complete poems – and not simply in the interests of whetting the appetite; time after time I found myself translating map references in terms of his lines. I can never again travel the suburbs of North Oxford without watching for a velvet-gowned, rose-pinned lady by a bus-stop; in Ireland the town of Mullingar will be evermore synonymous with the smell of garlic and fennel; in Camden Town, the façades of the terraces are enlivened by the consideration of a thousand business women taking baths.

The line drawings come from the pen of Leonora Ison, who

for many years illustrated the "Men and Buildings" pieces in the *Daily Telegraph*. Mrs. Ison captured Betjeman country in its heyday, at the time when he was at his most prolific, in the 1950s and 1960s, and Mrs. Ison echoed the world as he saw it, a sort of visualising amanuensis.

The photographs from archives are intended to convey the values whose disappearance John Betjeman has always regretted. Few living poets are so firmly welded to the immediate social past of their environment – the great historical or classical themes have never attracted him. Betjeman's dramas have always been played out at pavement or privet hedge level, and the world to which he harked back, the past world of his parents and his roots, emerges like a photograph album from his poems.

James Ravilious has photographed Betjeman country as it is now. Much of it still stands, outwardly unaltered, Magdalen College, St. Enodoc's Church in Cornwall, The Grove in Highgate. Sadly, Mr. Ravilious' pictures also define change: St. Saviour's Church, Aberdeen Park in North London is captured as it waits for – what? The demolisher's ball, the developer's pencil – who knows? But for one last time the source of one of the most important Betjeman poems has been preserved, if only two-dimensionally, and even the vandals have not been able to strip the abandoned church of its dignity. Horrors, alas, abound – the predicament of Slough and the City of London reinforce Betjeman's warning that we may judge the progress of our morality from the progress of our architecture.

Another century will judge John Betjeman more accurately – his work, with its roots so deeply planted in topographical and social observations, demands the objectivity of hindsight. My journeys have been personal ones, observations of the places he wrote in or about with a view to achieving a greater understanding of the English and their land – a place which I find extraordinarily different from what I had imagined. The air of calm settlement in Betjeman country is by far the most striking aspect: travelling through Berkshire and Surrey and the West Country the outstanding impression – heightened, admittedly, to an Irishman – is of a land which has never seen disruption or upheaval or invasion, a countryside that has had time to settle and calm itself and grow in stillness and peace.

The journeys were chosen in the way in which a casual traveller might move about – with a deliberate policy, too, of leaving room to embark on other future journeys. One day the Licorice Fields at Pontefract will provide hours of pleasure; I cannot wait to spend a weekend investigating the happenings at Kirkby with Muckby-cum-Sparrowby-cum-Spinx (which, as you know, "Is down a long lane in the county of Lincs"); and the click of the bat in the grounds of Cheltenham College will have to wait for decent cricket weather when "an ice and a macaroon" may yet again be brought forward on a boy's mortar-board acting as a tray.

The basic volumes consulted during travelling were *Summoned by Bells*, the blank verse autobiography first published in 1960, and the most recent edition of the *Collected Poems* (the volume published in 1979, containing *A Nip in the Air*). These books were chosen because they are the most prominent, comprehensive and generally available of John Betjeman's works, and they may thus prove useful should any reader desire, at the end of this book, to leave his armchair and wander off in the same spirit of enthusiastic enquiry to a fair in Pinner, or a crescent in Bath or a golf club in Surrey. And if you do discover "the cottage of The Agéd" from his poem "Blackfriars" in London, I shall envy you. For hours have I searched "By the shot tower near the chimneys, Off the road to Waterloo" with no success.

Which, perhaps, is a good thing. The most endearing result of all the travelling has not been the fact-finding, but the warm illusion. There are several doorways, crescents, lilac trees, gardens, which fit ideally into the picture conjured by the phrase "Betjeman country". And people, too – he wrote about them with affection and respect for their place in, their contribution to, the values of society's continuity. Betjeman country is a land of types – of buildings and people – who comfort by their very presence.

But Betjeman country has an even safer dimension – it is also a place in the mind, so that those who live there are permitted to preserve their individuality, are never made to feel satirised or mocked; it is finally a land whose geography is enhanced, expanded and immortalised by a poet's imaginings.

FRANK DELANEY
LONDON, SPRING 1983

Note: lest confusion arise regarding the spelling of the poet's surname, his father always used the traditional spelling, Betjemann, but his mother, responding to anticipated wartime antipathies, dropped one 'n'.

PART ONE

CHAPTER
ONE
HIGHGATE

I see black oak twigs outlined on the sky,
Red squirrels on the Burdett-Coutts estate.
I ask my nurse the question "Will I die?"
As bells from sad St. Anne's ring out so late,
"And if I do die, will I go to Heaven?"
Highgate at eventide. Nineteen-eleven.

John Betjeman was born, an only child, just outside Highgate in North London, on the slopes of Kentish Town, on Tuesday the 28th of August, 1906.

> Red cliffs arise. And up them service lifts
> Soar with the groceries to silver heights.
> Lissenden Mansions.

When John Betjeman was a baby, Lissenden Mansions was a better class of development. It still is, if slightly unsure of the fact. The opaque doorways murmur "Private". Tiles hallmark the corridors, fanlights and stained-glass, the advertisements of the paid-up. Ordered stillness – occasional young shouts outside, from the unexpected tennis court. An air of regulation prevails. The birthplace is unmarked – his stay here was so short. Soon after his birth the family moved, less than a mile away up Highgate West Hill.

> Here on the southern slope of Highgate Hill
> Red squirrels leap the hornbeams. Still I see
> Twigs and serrated leaves against the sky.

The lane, which became Highgate West Hill, was opened about 1700. On the left, as you climb, further residences, set high, back and apart above the road, and dignified in their individuality. On the right, thin, sad St. Anne's, whose incumbent leads a busy, perplexing life. "The Vicar," offers the noticeboard, "is usually available at The Vicarage for Baptism, Marriage and other matters."

Ernest and Bessie Betjemann rested on the slopes of society, a Dutch family name, sturdy middle-class furniture manufacturers. Through their semi-detached windows, across the climbing, winding road they gazed upon opulence – the Burdett-Coutts estate gleamed, large, leafy and benevolent. The Home Meadows, the Orchard, the Great Open Lawn, the Glade of Cedars, the Chestnut Terrace, the Forest Glade, the Beech Lawns, the Dell – sadly those gentle names would soon be sacrificed homogenously in the development addressed as the Holly Lodge Estate, effectively Highgate's garden city.

> The sunny silence was of Middlesex.
> Once a Delaunay-Belleville crawling up
> West Hill in bottom gear made such a noise
> As drew me from my dream-world out to watch
> That early motor-car attempt the steep.

Trees hide sober houses, red-tiled roofs, smokeless fuels. To the left the strong row of semi-detached villas which halts at Number 31, the early home of the poet.

The lawn was too small for a mowing-machine. Other recollections evoke a mauve jumper, of which he was "very proud", lovely, visited, explored shops, the smell of grass; there was birdsong – and centipedes, several centipedes, fearsome things, they

still haunt. Cushions of toffee were Golden Pats, he still dislikes licorice, other sweets actually tasted ill. Linoleum and carpet abutted, Bay Rum for the hair, an aura of spirits-of-salts disinfectant, bells rang far away. John, even then, played trains; even then Archibald, his bear, displayed unquestioning devotion. Outside the window, acorns, old husked tins with labels peeling and fading, leaves with strange shapes, a stick: in the ordinary is the extraordinary.

Pause at the crest of West Hill and look backward. An earlier chronicler, James Boswell, travelling from Scotland, came upon Highgate Hill too, and had a view of London. "I was all life and joy, I gave three huzzas and went briskly in."

Approached from all sides by hills, therefore departed from down steep slopes, one may always feel a little exalted by Highgate. Donnish trees, tall good houses, iron gates to brick parthenons, a courtly village, head to one side, quiet with confidence. It may even have missed its vocation – it has the muscles of a country market town. At the top, West Hill continues into

Highgate High Street – a tradesman's entrance. And The Grove, broad and stately on your immediate left, is Highgate's polished front door.

Pause. By your left shoulder, a single lodge, and beyond, a great brick mock-chateau, built of Sunlight Soap in the days when Sir Arthur Crosfield made it. Diagonally from your right shoulder, beyond some shy triangles of grass, is the Flask, younger than it looks: 1663 on the plaque is a reversed boast and a local joke. Behind you, St. Michael's Church, a landmark for David Copperfield, and inside, stained glass by Evie Hone. Doorscrapers, fading crests, buttresses and another puzzling notice-board: "Baptisms, marriages by arrangement". And – funerals?

When John was small he was invited to a children's party, "to the great big house in The Grove". On the way he passed Number 3, The Grove, where Coleridge, ailing and opiate, came to rest in 1823 and died in 1834. Hazlitt visited him there and said, "He talked on forever and you wished him to talk on forever." Keats, from over the Heath at Hampstead, met Coleridge too. "Let me carry away the memory, Coleridge, of having pressed your hand!" Coleridge watched him go and murmured, "There is death in that hand." The Grove was further equal to John Drinkwater, Gladys Cooper, J. B. Priestley, Yehudi Menuhin, but although the party was a success, cakes and ices and jelly, little John Betjeman was not.

> Can I forget my delight at the conjuring show?
> And wasn't I proud that I was the last to go?
> Too overexcited and pleased with myself to know
> That the words I heard my hostess's mother employ
> To a guest departing, would ever diminish my joy,
> I WONDER WHERE JULIA FOUND THAT STRANGE, RATHER
> COMMON LITTLE BOY?

In The Grove now, the faces of the tall houses are veiled by cow parsley, limes and horse chestnuts. Stiff society ladies, corseted by railings, assured by doorways, each residence aloof and careful, hands by its sides; this is where John Betjeman first encountered the power of the drawing-room – which was to go on hurting.

> Phone for the fish-knives, Norman
> As Cook is a little unnerved;
> You kiddies have crumpled the serviettes
> And I must have things daintily served.

Every morning, John Betjeman climbed West Hill, walked along The Grove, crossed Hampstead Lane and went to Byron House Co-Educational Preparatory School in North Grove.

> O Peggy Purey-Cust, how pure you were:
> My first and purest love, Miss Purey-Cust!
> Satchel on back I hurried up West Hill
> To catch you on your morning walk to school,
> Your nanny with you and your golden hair
> Streaming like sunlight.

The Purey-Custs lived near the top of West Hill, at Number

82, and invited little John Betjeman to tea, a much happier occasion. From their house – as from the gardens of The Grove – sylvania lies beneath, with, elsewhere, the old buildings of the City and the dome of St. Paul's. Mrs. Purey-Cust smiled at John from a sofa and her beam became part of the view, part of his young love, part of Peggy, part of all future dreams.

> Your ice-blue eyes, your lashes long and light,
> Your sweetly freckled face and turned-up nose
> So haunted me that all my loves since then
> Have had a look of Peggy Purey-Cust.
> Along The Grove, what happy, happy steps

Under the limes I took to Byron House,
And blob-work, weaving, carpentry and art,
Walking with you; and with what joy returned.

Byron House is gone now. Nowhere on the unrefined new
pavements is the little ghost of Peggy Purey-Cust, the herald
angel, the seeds of love of all the Myfanwys and Joan Hunter
Dunns. From Byron House he went for one year to nearby
Southwood Lane where Highgate Junior School then stood.
(Gone too – it was pulled down half a century later and replaced
by the kind of building he has always campaigned against.)

During his interview for Highgate Junior School he failed to
disclose to the great headmaster how many half-crowns in a
pound. But compensation came – from poetry, and a real poet,
teaching, in the school.

The American master, Mr. Eliot,
That dear good man, with Prufrock in his head
And Sweeney waiting to be agonized.

Betjeman's procession through Highgate is his seed-bed. In
the rich houses of The Grove he suffered social distinction. In
the little desks of Byron House he found his princess. In the
ink stains of Highgate Junior School he encountered his muse,
and bound his early jottings and handed them confidently to
the kindlily unseeing T. S. Eliot.

On the posters outside the school Lord Kitchener wanted
everybody, and another Betjeman element was being formed –
fear.

"Betjeman's a German spy –
Shoot him down and let him die:
Betjeman's a German spy,
A German spy, a German spy."

He calls the bullies' names still, a frightened couplet: "Robson and Ibbotson / Ibbotson and Robson", but they caught him
at cold Swain's Lane.

There in a holly bush they threw me down,
Pulled off my shorts, and laughed and ran away;
And, as I struggled up, I saw grey brick,
The cemetery railings and the tombs.

Is there *always* somebody in a cemetery? An American count-

ing the rings on the family tree? An author in search of a character? An old lover pursuing an anniversary? Workmen, yoricking about this sprawling place. Wide, and powerfully still, bisected banked and staggered by Swain's Lane, a miniature skyline, Highgate Cemetery was gothically intended and designed, with cupolas and sepulchres and walks and bell towers. John Galsworthy buried his mythical Forsytes here – tourists seek their tombs. Living myths too – Rossetti's lovely, lonely wife, Elizabeth Siddal, died of laudanum after two years of marriage. Her grieving husband Dante buried their courting poems; seven years later he exhumed them at midnight by the light of a bonfire. And Karl Marx, leonine, sphinx-like, and avenues of angels, draped stone urns, columns broken off in their prime – this is a startling place, an unevenly unkempt place, where the most recent bereavement forms a temporary unexpected oasis of clay.

> He would have liked to say goodbye,
> Shake hands with many friends,
> In Highgate now his finger-bones
> Stick through his finger-ends.

In *Old Lights For New Chancels* published in 1940, Betjeman's terrified melancholy is personalised. His father used an ear trumpet, took John on long silent walks, is buried beneath a red obelisk in Highgate Cemetery.

> And when he could not hear me speak
> He smiled and looked so wise
> That now I do not like to think
> Of maggots in his eyes.

John left Highgate Junior School as unsuccessfully as he had begun. He was sent, aged eleven, to the Dragon School in Oxford in 1917. The family left West Hill and moved to Church Street, Chelsea. John, unhappy, wrote anxiously from school. On his next holiday the regret set in – it congealed subsequently, and his soul stayed on in Highgate.

> I missed the climb
> By garden walls and fences where a stick,
> Dragged on the palings, clattered to my steps,
> I missed the smell of trodden leaves and grass. . .

And all the good people – Mr. Dimmock, Mrs. Bunny, Aunt Polly, Mrs. Pitt who brought bananas. And prayers, stained-glass, distant bells, trains, loneliness; Betjeman country begins in this elevated citadel of North London.

And did he ever really leave? The man in the caverned, avenued antiquarian bookshop of Fisher and Sperr recalls the grown-up John Betjeman kneeling and crawling on the floor to see the books on the lowest shelves. In the white-fronted peace of the Highgate Literary and Scientific Institution he has spoken of Coleridge. He has climbed this hill of poets, this little parnassus and cried how lucky he was to have been born where Keats and Coleridge were inspired.

Highgate, once a small sunlit clearing in the Middlesex forest, has been growing for seven centuries into a mature, well-bred, residential crossroads settlement. Geoffrey and Anne Lewis sell flowers beside a clothes shop called "Partners". A. J. Foulston is a state-registered chiropodist. Sweet Lorraine Ltd. is registered too – her good offices are in the High Street. In the Highgate Literary and Scientific Institution there is to be a Grand Quiz for the Isla Merry Mug.

Prickett and Ellis, Sturt and Tivendale offer properties – never houses – in Hillcrest and Broadlands. In the Prince of Wales ask for games at the bar – nine men's morris, solitaire, crib, darts, draughts, dominoes. A coin in a charity box tells fortunes: "You will get what you want with patience."

In the stationer's window a lady is required to take temporary charge of Retired Clergy. (Temporary?) Painting – A Good Job. Fair Prices. A Turkish rug for sale. $4\frac{1}{4}$ yards good quality, dark orange velveteen. Chintz covers in pure Irish linen. Set of matching tiles.

In Betjeman country Highgate is the fountainhead. Class consciousness, fear of violence, death, doubt and sin – all were pupped in Highgate and these dogs pursued him down the years. And the love of ideal women was born, the comfort of red brick, the freedom of leaves and trains, the pull of verse.

> For myself,
> I knew as soon as I could read and write
> That I must be a poet. Even today,
> When all the way from Cambridge comes a wind
> To blow the lamps out every time they're lit,
> I know that I must light up mine again.

There was one last hound to haunt him. He did not, despite entreating glances and wise forecasts, succeed to the family furniture business. His father, sire and foreman all at once, was wounded, mortally. The poet's largest debt was guilt, never paid off, compounded.

And now when I behold, fresh-published, new,
A further volume of my verse, I see
His kind grey eyes look woundedly at mine,
I see his workmen seeking other jobs,
And that red granite obelisk that marks
The family grave in Highgate Cemetery
Points an accusing finger to the sky.

CHAPTER
TWO
CORNWALL

The wideness which the lark-song gives the sky
Shrinks at the clang of sea-birds sailing by
Whose notes are tuned to days when seas are high.

From to-day's calm, the lane's enclosing green
Leads inland to a usual Cornish scene –
Slate cottages with sycamore between,

Small fields and tellymasts and wires and poles
With, as the everlasting ocean rolls,
Two chapels built for half a hundred souls.

Cornwall is Betjeman's holy well. The small parishes, the gleaming beaches, villages low by harbours or high by crossroads, the memory of friends – here they all come together. Cornwall was the genesis of more than a quarter of *Summoned by Bells*. In several other poems the little churches – architectural souvenirs – the musical names of local saints, the high windy skies, the slabbed slate cliffs, all search and find him, and his melancholy spirit ebbs and flows with the tides.

> An only child, deliciously apart,
> Misunderstood and not like other boys,
> Deep, dark and pitiful I saw myself
> In my mind's mirror, every step I took
> A fascinating study to the world.

When small John Betjeman first crossed into Cornwall, the family drove from the station to Trebetherick in a horse-brake – the parish's only motor-car baulked at the hills. Oil lamps and candles lit the village windows: the Betjemans were foreigners in a place where London – Devon even – was an adventure away. (One who did venture forth returned, agog that London was "all under a glass roof" – he had not risked it beyond Paddington Station.)

Inland from Trebetherick, to the east and the north, are the villages which became his private shrines, Chapel Amble, St. Minver, St. Endellion, St. Kew, St. Tudy, St. Teath; by the coast, Pentire, Portquin, Port Isaac – and on up, past the slate quarries of Delabole to Tintagel and Boscastle. Often the swooping roads are narrow corridors between high banks. Sometimes, through gateways, by farmyards, the fields slope down to the sea. The hedges and small trees are hunched like the shoulders of old men, bent away from the centuries of prevailing winds.

The signposts read like a smuggler's shanty – Trevalga, Trewarmett, Tremail, Trewalder, Trelights, Tremaine. Fields, sheep-sprinkled, plane steeply down to the cliffs, where rocks in the tide, old fangs, menace the shore. Churches and chapels are as customary as neighbours, the round-faced Celtic crosses stand by the roadside consolingly, and Button and Mutton of Wadebridge offer properties in advantageous positions.

> Waves full of treasure then were rowing up the beach,
> Ropes around our mackintoshes, waders warm and dry,
> We waited for the wreckage to come swirling into reach,
> Ralph, Vasey, Alastair, Biddy, John and I.

Cornwall yields up Betjeman, vivid and immediate, in all his loneliness, his fears, his religious supplication, his wistful yearning for old and warm times. His spirit prayed and fasted in this wild place, with its yellows and greys and browns and brooding blacks and bright whites. From violent family arguments and pools of bruised silence he fled, and sought forgiveness in remote, damp-walled churches which echoed to the clattering of bats and the ticking of beetles.

> In the cool shade of interlacing boughs,
> I found St. Ervan's partly ruined church.
> Its bearded Rector, holding in one hand
> A gong-stick, in the other hand a book,
> Struck, while he read, a heavy-sounding bell,
> Hung from an elm bough by the churchyard gate.
> "Better come in. It's time for Evensong."

And tea later, and barely furnished rooms, an apiary and discussion:

> . . . "And I suppose
> You think religion's mostly singing hymns
> And feeling warm and comfortable inside?"
> And he was right: most certainly I did.

But outside the womb, haunting, primeval Celtic Cornwall came thundering in, shadows and force, in this land where creatures shamble over the fields at night, where the morning may divulge something awful.

> Thick with sloe and blackberry, uneven in the light,
> Lonely ran the hedge, the heavy meadow was remote,
> The oldest part of Cornwall was the wood as black as night,
> And the pheasant and the rabbit lay torn open at the throat.

Down by the shore the blowholes boom, menace, racking apprehension, a song of shipwrecked souls cast up at lonely, worrying Tregardock. The cliff path to Tregardock is glassed with water from thin wandering streams, the descent is steep, marshy, unfriendly. Gorse warns from both sides, a white house stands aloof, bow-windowed, possessive. The land is smooth with farmed care, public footpaths etch tangents, drawing away from the sea. This is a hostile shore, there are shadows. In later years, wounded by a critic – "journalism full of hate" – Betjeman returned to these "gigantic slithering shelves of slate". It was October and misty; he was downcast, enervated, suicidal.

And I on my volcano edge
Exposed to ridicule and hate
Still do not dare to leap the ledge
And smash to pieces on the slate.

The climb back to the lane is stiff. The roof of the white farm house is nunned with pigeons, barnacled to the wall a rusty mill wheel; in an open shed an aged tractor sits, cannibalised and demoted.

From Tregardock, turn to St. Teath, whose name rhymes with "death", birthplace of Captain Bligh of the *Bounty* – but a comforting and friendly village, at a high crossroads. Proceed

westwards to St. Endellion, a parish much ported: Port Isaac, Portquin, Port Gaverne and forward, take the coast road by Pentireglaze and Pentire down to the Doom Bar – sandbanked revenge on mariners for a slain mermaid – then on past Polzeath and Trebetherick on the way to the church of St. Enodoc.

"Sunday Afternoon Service in St. Enodoc Church, Cornwall" is a matter of local knowledge: St. Enodoc is hidden, near Daymer Bay, between Rock and Trebetherick. From either place, long lanes and long walks hide the way to this quaint, dim church, snug among the dunes with a little spire like an elf's hat. John Betjeman walked from the beach at Daymer Bay. There is access too, from the golf-club side, to Bray Hill – along

a scarcely signposted lane and when eventually the entrance materialises it has been reserved for golfers who do things by halves from the tenth tee. By the white stones on the fairway, respectfully skirting the green, the church, walled and hedged from the imminent sea, huddles peacefully down in the hillocks. "Sinkininny Church", laughed the locals, when the sand drifted over it and the visiting prelate had to be lowered through the roof. "Stand with your back to the church," exhorts the scribe of the parish of St. Minver, of which St. Enodoc is the north chapelry – "and look towards the open sea over Daymer Bay. In pre-historic times you would have been looking through a forest where wild animals were roaming. We know this because in 1857 a great gale shifted the sand and twelve feet below high-water mark, the stumps and roots of oaks, yews and hazelnut trees were found with horns and teeth of deer and other animals. The sand covered them again and they are no longer visible."

Enodoc the hermit, though, is not as well documented. Did he have a cell by a spring under the church's rood screen? He may have baptised his converts in Jesus Well, to the south-east, where local people supplicate a whooping-cough cure. His church is now entered through a lych-gate, roofed like an inverted boat. Along the path, a dozen, thirteen paces, towards the door – then sharp left, to the perimeter of the little church-yard, between mourned Mablys and Burtons and Heygates and Mercers and Uniackes. Sheltered beneath the boundary hedge is a slate-coloured oblong upright slab: Mabel Bessie Betjeman who departed this life the 13th of December 1952 aged 74 years:

> Her wit, her gaiety, the jokes we shared,
> The love for her that waited underneath,
> I kept in check;

Inside the church, an answering echo: her husband is commemorated by a tablet. Edward Ernest Betjemann of Undertown in this parish, Born 22nd October, 1872. Died 22nd June, 1934. "I feared my father, loved my mother more."

The flowers, in the Norman porch, came from the St. Enodoc Flower Roster – "Mrs. Davis, Mrs. Roome, Mrs. Seeley."

> My eyes, recovering in the sudden shade,
> Discern the long-known little things within –
> A map of France in damp above my pew.

In a tiny recess, a truncated transept, the rope pulls a ship-wrecked bell – beached a century and more ago. High cushions on the chair exalt the organist. The window over the communion

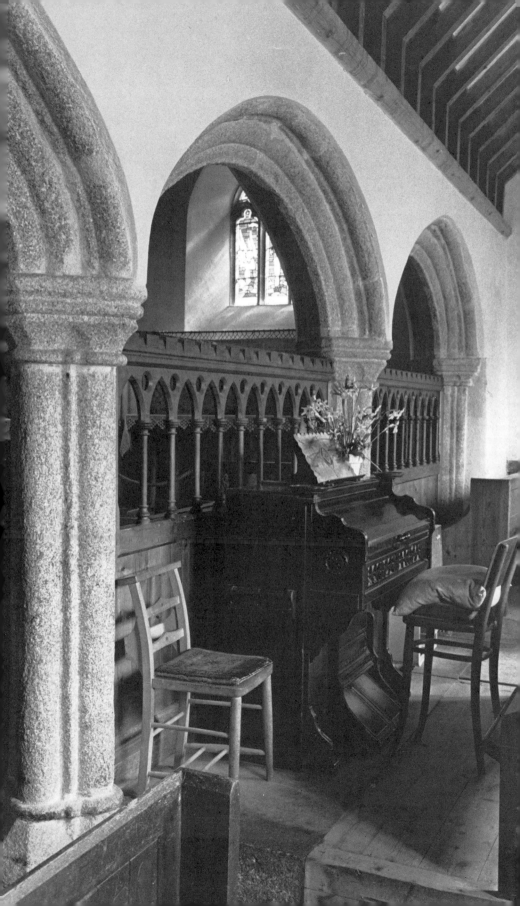

table was raised "To the Glory of God and in Loving Memory of Theophilus Hoskin of Bray" – in that order.

> The modest windows palely glazed with green,
> The smooth slate floor, the rounded wooden roof,
> The Norman arch, the cable-moulded font –
> All have a humble and West Country look.

Hassocks, hand-embroidered, and diligent hymn-books are tidied through the pews. The larksong from the high field to the south sweetens the afternoon stillness: scrape of footstep, another visitor. A tablet regrets the death of 2nd Lieut. Ronald Chard Roseveare, of the 1st Somerset Light Infantry, "who fell in action near Ypres, Aug. 8, 1916, aged 19".

The unknown sailors, buried without, were cast up, like driftwood, into St. Enodoc's yard. John Mably of Trebetherick and

William Mably, Yeoman, are interred behind and beneath ancient stones.

> The tide is high and a sleepy Atlantic sends
>   Exploring ripple on ripple down Polzeath shore,
> And the gathering dark is full of the thought of friends
>   I shall see no more.

John Betjeman still retreats to Cornwall, even though Trebetherick has been barbered into small holiday and retirement suburbs. White and removed, with ilex and conifer, the bungalows stand behind St. Enodoc and his golf club, gleaming over superannuated lawns. To bewail such "progress" he invented, in prose, the village of Trepolport: "On the way to the churchtown I pass the Squire's drive and see that his house has become a country hotel, and the once trim garden round the house where

the church fête was held has that half-tended look, neither municipal, nor private, peculiar to hotel gardens . . . Now look up at the cliffs. Row after row of new bungalows climb the sides . . . The inn has . . . done itself up Elizabethan with diamond lattice, and has a bar named 'The Starboard Lights' in deference to the small-boat craze. No fishermen live in the little cottages any more and by October these little houses are empty until they are tenanted again next summer by holidaymakers . . ."

Trepolport is Tintagel with Camelot flats, B & B at Halcyon, King Arthur's café, and a neon sign, "Excali-Bar with Bar Snacks and Entertainment". And even on the escape route from Trepolport/Tintagel there lurks a Cornish Pixey house, all gnomes and rancid concrete. "With my memories of what Cornwall once was," wept Betjeman in sorrow and in anger, "I cannot help wishing for a higher spring tide than any high tide the Cornish coast has ever known."

In Betjeman country, his Cornwall corner remains a refuge, a place apart, first seen, all those years ago, through a train window, haunted woods, hedges spiced with fennel, glimpsed slate, Atlantic rollers, gulls in the sky, oyster-catchers on the beach – exhilarating, inspiring.

> But somewhere, somewhere underneath the dunes,
> Somewhere among the cairns or in the caves
> The Celtic saints would come to me, the ledge
> Of time we walk on, like a thin cliff-path
> High in the mist, would show the precipice.

Along the line of life, somewhere, somewhere, John Betjeman became pusillanimous. Was it the physical size, the pain of being small? Or disappointing his father, or unable, Englishly, to speak love to his mother? Timidity, lack of confidence and the knowledge that being able to make people laugh buys a ticket too – as they all appeared in his student years, they appear in his poems. But in Cornwall there is a different voice. He is given strength by the surroundings, he is rounded by the waves.

Society gouged him, his small physique denied him immediate stature, his father's disappointment seamed and scored him. But in his Cornwall, and only there, he was comforted. The pagan echoes and the intimate saints excited and nourished him, the landscape and the little churches rewarded him, the history and the sense of prayer restored him.

> The sky widens towards Cornwall. A sense of sea
> Hangs in the lichenous branches and still there's light.

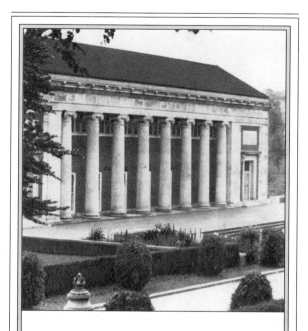

CHAPTER
THREE
MARLBOROUGH

Luxuriating backwards in the bath,
I swish the warmer water round my legs
Towards my shoulders, and the waves of heat
Bring those five years of Marlborough through to me,
In comfortable retrospect: "Thank God
I'll never have to go through them again."

John Betjeman went to Marlborough College in 1920, left it in 1925, was variously happy and miserable there and never thereafter coped with his own ambivalence towards the place.

> As with my toes I reach towards the tap
> And turn it to a trickle, stealing warm
> About my tender person, comes a voice,
> An inner voice that calls, "Be fair! be fair!
> It was not quite as awful as you think."

An octogenarian citizen of Marlborough, a maid at the school then – she was seventeen and domestic staff were not allowed to speak to the boys – recalls that Betjeman was "small and plump with a fat face".

He would emerge into the barred wells of B House – can it be true that the architect specialised in H.M. Prison designs? – "spouting poetry". During the week the boys wore black suits, with white stiff collars; in summer they added boaters. He was,

...he recalls, a "silly boy" and others pulled his leg about his poems, which he chanted while walking round and round. Louis MacNeice, the poet from Ulster, was at Marlborough with Betjeman, and in his unfinished autobiography he also offers something less than adulation. "Betjeman was not altogether the suppressed and retiring character one might suppose from reading the Marlborough chapter in *Summoned by Bells*. He was to be seen bowling a hoop through the school court with a green feather behind his ear; and the adjustable sallies at the expense of the deaf bandmaster/invigilator of which he gives a sample were usually coined by him." And freshly minted for the purposes of autobiography.

> I see the tall Memorial Reading Room,
> Which smelt of boots and socks and water-pipes,
> Its deaf invigilator on his throne –
> *"Do you tickle your arse with a feather, Mr. Purdick?"*
> *"What?"*
> *"Particularly nasty weather, Mr. Purdick!"*
> *"Oh."*
> And, as the water cools, the Marlborough terms
> Form into seasons.

Marlborough College was founded in 1843, once a castle, then a country house, carriages, a circular lawn, Lady Hertford, then a great inn. A grand place, far enough from London to be amusing, close enough to be convenient, deep enough in Wiltshire to eschew commuters, to claim kinship with this rich, rolling country, blue-green grass, early summer roadside corridors of Queen Anne lace, chalk walks, enigmatic downs. The ley lines in Wiltshire, they say, those invisible magic wires, connect the old stone circles, Avebury and Stonehenge, like the stations on some secret cabalistic railway. This part of north Wiltshire provided royal hunting in the forests, thatched villages, small towns with wide streets, mansions, prosperity firmly planted between the River Kennet and the upper reaches of the Thames.

The small, organised town of Marlborough maintains its reputation for streets, "the widest in Britain", the locals assert; a gratifying high street, certainly, and wide, and sloping, and Georgian, and belled, and arched. A stage-coach town, this, inns and the memories of ostlers' yards, and old timbers and churches, St. Peter's, standing firm at the conclusion of the high street, offset by the town hall which pretends to be older than its rebuilt 1903. "An ill-looking place enough", said William Cobbett, but that was before the college was established.

In front of the brick façade the quadrangle opens to the west:

on one side an incongruous architectural mix, a high, glassed modern dining-hall, abutted by Queen Anne houses (surprisingly, working parts of the school) and, directly facing them, a small colonnade, then a theatre, a library and at the logical conclusion of the quadrangle a chapel. Breakfast begins at a quarter to eight, Assembly every third Monday at quarter to nine, fifteen houses in all, and in the upper reaches a pool of girls who board in dormitories more out-of-bounds than bounds could ever be.

Within the houses, the boys improvise upon the basic order, rebelling with a poster, or a sports pin-up, or a cricket bat swaggering in the confines of a cubicle. Unexpected good taste in colour and decor erupts in small revolutions against legendary buff-painted walls. The stone steps sway towards the middle, worn down by countless pounding shoes: brass, old fuse-boxes, railings and a billiard table in an atrium indicate that a misspent youth is not what it was. In the public exchange between master and boy, bipartisan courtesy is the order of the day. The classrooms resemble debating concourses – squares or rectangles of tables over which an air of pleasing reason prevails.

In a corridor a boy in an afternoon-off white sweater leans against the wall with a deferential carelessness, as only a senior schoolboy can. He is waiting to attend a *viva* – not at all nervous, he insists, but his *voce* trembles a little. On the notice-board by the museum block, Eton and Charterhouse advertise athletic competitions in the forthcoming months. In an L-shaped room nearby, past the brick courts and the lintel with Greek lettering, in a classroom derived from an old stable block, John Betjeman trembled at the character formation of the public school system which, in preparation for life, gave boys power over other smaller, weaker boys.

> Before the master came for evening prep
> The captains entered at official pace
> And, walking down the alley-way of desks,
> Beat on their level lids with supple canes.
> This was the sign for new boys to arise,
> To pick up paper, apple-cores and darts
> And fill huge baskets with the muck they found;
> Then, wiping hands upon grey handkerchiefs
> And trousers, settle down to Latin prose.
> Upper School captains had the power to beat:
> Maximum six strokes, usually three.

In Betjeman's time the boy-rulers of Marlborough held their court in a vast, cold, high-roofed building known as Upper School. Evening prep occurred in Upper School for an hour, from a quarter past seven. The huge room was heated by two coal fireplaces, Big Fire and Little Fire. At Big Fire the four school captains congregated, each with his chosen three friends. These sixteen boys were exceptional only by seniority or athletic prowess and Little Fire, over a hundred from the junior slopes in the Senior School, trembled in their pathway, and huddled round the less exclusive fireplace. Each evening the twelve boys who were the captains' friends indulged in elaborate horseplay to keep the captains and their canes out of Upper School. But the heroes always came through, caning on the least pretext.

> My frequent crime was far too many books,
> So that my desk lid would not shut at all:
> "Come to Big Fire, then, Betjeman, after prep."

Caning held fewer terrors than other Upper School pastimes. Once a term a boy, for equally trivial reasons, would be singled out for "Put in the Basket".

Perhaps he sported coloured socks too soon,
Perhaps he smarmed his hair with scented oil,
Perhaps he was "immoral" or a thief.

No matter what the reason a silent cloud descended upon this
newly manufactured pariah. The enormous wastepaper basket,
full of pencil shavings, orange peel, discarded paper, dried mud
from shoes, broken nibs, floor fluff, was dragged forward, fol-
lowed by the white, shaking victim.

They surrounded him,
Pulled off his coat and trousers, socks and shoes
And, wretched in his shirt, they hoisted him
Into the huge waste-paper basket; then
Poured ink and treacle on his head. With ropes
They strung the basket up among the beams,
And as he soared I only saw his eyes
Look through the slats at us who watched below.

Frequently the boy left Marlborough at the end of the term.
There was little other choice – he was ostracised because he had
been humiliated; the image which most boys retained of him
was creeping out of Upper School, holding his trousers and his
tears. For several terms afterwards John Betjeman, threatened
with the Basket, hid away, crept about, fearful of having his
character formed. Upper School is extinct now; the building has
disappeared, Marlborough is a gentler, more civilised place.
Except in a poet's memory: Louis MacNeice applied his most
concentrated vitriol to the Basket. "The masters considered this
a fine old tradition, and any boy who had been basketed was
under a cloud for the future. Because the boys have an innate
sense of justice, anyone they basket must be really undesirable.
Government of the mob, by the mob, and for the mob."
John Betjeman remains frightened. "It was the most dreadful
thing, frightful. I think it was one of the things which most gave
me my persecution mania."

In the library at Marlborough, a neat and quiet small hall, tables
the colour of light cork stand between stacks of books. Boys,
the occasional girl, sitting perfectly still, try to force their concentration into ever longer spans. At the top, at a raised desk,
overseeing and alert as a clerk in a Dickensian counting-house,
but benign, helpful, encouraging, sits the librarian. In his care
rest the earliest published works: in the *Marlburian*, the 29th
of June, 1922, "J.B." wrote in memory of a dead Irish friend,
John O'Regan.

I took the paper up and read –
Sadly I laid it down,
And thought of him now lying dead
In the dear little town:

And back came ancient memories,
And back came ancient days;
His many little kindnesses,
His playful Irish ways;

The fun, the fives, the games once played,
That game we were to play
On a small ball-court he had laid
Out Killycoonagh way.

Impulsive, sometimes hasty? Yes,
But O, none ever heard
Him even in his hastiness
Speak an unkindly word.

Good-bye, old friend, passed into rest,
A soldier at his post,
Sure here round all thou loved'st best
Shall hover still thy ghost.

Later, John Betjeman's other literary activities at school suggested fortunate improvement. The legendary adolescent conflict between the corps of the physique and the dedicatees of the soul – eventually the "hearties" and "aesthetes" of Oxford

– broke over Betjeman in Marlborough, and he placed himself, by his eccentricities and esotericisms, in an unnumbered box among the aesthetes. Their unnamed leader was Anthony Blunt, later of multifarious reputation. The aesthetes had their revenge on the college establishment by publishing the *Heretick*. Betjeman contributed frequently to it, in verse and in prose, much of which heralds his emergent strain of satirical whimsy.

In one piece, *Dinner of Old Marlburian Centipede Farmers in Unyamezi, S.A.*, he lampooned all contributions to school magazines from old boys. "I take up my pen to write about this dinner to any boys of the old school who think of taking up our work; we had six courses. Although the shanty where we met is 100 miles from any other habitation the table was decorated with O.M. colours and we had a full attendance. Present (the numbers after name and house are the miles traversed to get to the dinner): Chairman – X. Jones A6 (485), Y. Brown B5 (3000). The chairman said after the dinner, 'Life here is no mere routine: in the early morning the coolies (*native servants*) carry (*bring*) crarg (*hot*) aeiou (*water*). During the day it is too hot to work, so there is nothing to do but wait for tiffin (*luncheon*) and then to rest until wiffin (*tea*) after which it is time to prepare for spiffin (*supper*).'" And the letter concludes wickedly, "I advise all boys who like an open-air life and who won't grumble at a bit of hard work to come and join us here."

Other artistic endeavours appeared in contributions to the *Heretick*'s printed, would-be dramas, which were filled with Fast Lads and Plain Boys whose voices are raised in praise of super cars and athletes.

(The chorus rises higher and higher until it becomes a scream . . . Finally a route of *PRODIGIES* enter. They dance round the Recording Angel singing.)

PRODIGIES' SONG

Bright blue skies, and now on the river
Laziness lies in punt and pillows,
Wandering winds make willow leaves shiver,
But what care we for the wind in the willows?
What care we for the meadows deep
And the gentle Kennet's silvery hazes?
Life is only a muddle heap
Of adjectival phrases.

Other odd poems appeared: even in a canon of work

renowned for idiosyncracy, Betjeman's published juvenilia is egregious.

> Here comes Muffin-man down the street,
> With trays and baize and bell,
> Calling and bawling and shuffling his feet,
> And carrying muffins as well.
>
> Muffin Man! Muffin Man! Little you'll stay
> The smart my heart must know,
> At seeing, and fleeing unwilling, away
> From the muffins I long for so.
>
> Muffins oh! Muffins oh! Time was when
> (How glad, yet sad, to say)
> Greedy, and needy, I gobbled up ten
> And practic'lly passed away.
>
> Muffin Man! Muffin Man! Saying to me!
> (I know your low design)
> "Stop fretting, forgetting the pains to be."
> All right! I'll purchase nine.

*   *   *

Caprice excepted, Marlborough gave the early Betjeman his sense of direction. Fear, death, aestheticism, Victoriana, architecture, eccentric behaviour – they swelled at school, subjects in the eventual Betjeman's poetic curriculum. Fear was a general thing, terror of the fascist hearties and captains, fear was a mood associated permanently with regimen.

> Doom! Shivering doom! Inexorable bells
> To early school, to chapel, school again:
> Compulsory constipation, hurried meals
> Bulked out with Whipped Cream Walnuts from the town.
> At first there was the dread of breaking rules –
> "Betjeman, you know that new boys musn't show
> Their hair below the peak of college caps:
> Stand still and have your face slapped." "Sorry, Jones."
> The dread of beatings! Dread of being late!
> And, greatest dread of all, the dread of games!

In the *Heretick* he wrote a most curious prose piece called "Death", an inconclusive story of sorrow and faith and haunting by a heavenly priest wearing white robes, who drew Betjeman to the mortuary chapel in the cemetery. "I saw him, his robes waving in the wind, walking towards the corner where the workhouse folk are buried. I longed for the man, in a way I loved him.

"In the workhouse corner the woman on the terrace was clinging to a white cross. He touched her. She fell limply, and gently he raised her and they seemed to go up to heaven, fainter and fainter in the mist." The piece concludes abruptly and inexplicably: "This is a silly story with no point in it. Do not think of it any more; shout for your house on the touch line, turn your back to his Garden, you will soon have enough of polished granite, a white cross or a broken pillar."

Other boys provided early love, harmless and idealistic, cycling through the countryside, sitting in long grass on top of the downs, tolerating even a love of motor-cars. Aestheticism flourished under the art teacher's tutelage –

Glory was in me as I tried to paint
The stretch of meadow and the line of downs,
Putting in buttercups in bright gamboge,
Ultramarine and cobalt for the sky,
With blotting-paper, while the page was wet,
For cloud effects.

John Betjeman cut chapel in Marlborough, preferred to call verse aloud up the stairwells of B House, listened to papers on Cubism read by Anthony Blunt. He sketched trees, landscapes and Wiltshire cottages, collected Victorian printed ephemera, annuals, anthologies of poetry with engravings. He was capable of telling all his fellows that he was about to cycle into Swindon "to look at a train" and Louis MacNeice's pen-picture drew "John Betjeman writing nonsense on his typewriter or polishing

his leather books with boot-polish. John Betjeman at that time looked like a will-o'-the-wisp with Latin blood in it. His face was the colour of peasoup and his eyes were soupy too and his mouth was always twisting sideways in a mocking smile and he had a slight twist in his speech which added a tang to his mimicries, syncopating the original just as a slightly rippling sheet of water jazzes the things reflected in it. He was a brilliant mimic but also a mine of useless information and a triumphant misfit."

Marlborough today is still a quiet town, peaceful in the Wiltshire sun; the trees, the old forests and the downs still converge, and at the end of the "hot High Street" the college is brick and dignified and withdrawn but not aloof. Perhaps Frazer-Nash motor-cars no longer rev in the roads – "Gosh, what an engine" – but on free afternoons, students still buy ices in the High Street, or take Sunday walks – "the smell of trodden leaves beside the Kennet".

After five years, John Betjeman left Marlborough College in 1925: by that time he had assimilated the place, had formed some meaning, a loving friendship, an attitude towards the school, towards himself. In turn, the place had given him freedom of expression, the opportunity to mix with superior, formative minds, with boys whom he found intellectually courageous, with masters who gave his eccentric instincts some free rein. And by the time he was finished with Marlborough, he had, in the *Heretick* in 1924, given a strong indication of the shape of poems to come.

> The happy haunt of typists common, pert,
> "We're in the country now!" they say,
>   and wear
> Tweed clothes, and let the wind disturb
>   their hair,
> And carry ash sticks. "Don't be silly, Gert!
> Afraid of cows?" "Oh Elsie, mind my skirt,
> It will get muddy." "Oh just look down
>   there
> A factory . . ." "O dearest, how they dare
> To ruin all the country with their dirt!"
> And Gert and Elsie's cottage – "Just too
>   sweet"
> With rustic furniture, no bath, no drains
> But still it is so countrified: A friend
> Can sleep upon the sofa. And they eat
> Off pottery (hand painted). Oh! the pains
> And saving for their game of let's pretend!

CHAPTER
FOUR
OXFORD

At the time of evening when cars run sweetly,
    Syringas blossom by Oxford gates.
In her evening velvet with a rose pinned neatly
    By the distant bus-stop a don's wife waits.

John Betjeman has written about Oxford lovingly and extensively. Close to a fifth of *Summoned by Bells* is devoted to the city; other poems, less personal, are equally affectionate. In 1925 he went joyfully up to Magdalen, where he wore extravagant cravats, embroidered waistcoats, hand-made shoes. He was small, plump and amusing; much beloved of the female students – and still mischievously proud of the fact. He did very little academic work: during his three years he edited an undergraduate publication called *Cherwell*, he invented a cocktail of advocaat and sherry. He smoked Balkan Sobranie cigarettes, he quarrelled with his tutor C. S. Lewis. And – "first steps in learning how to be a guest" – he dined frequently at the expansive country houses of wealthy friends or in witty donnish rooms.

> A dozen oysters and a dryish hock;
> Claret and *tournedos*; a *bombe surprise* . . .
> The fusillade of phrases ("I'm a man
> More dined against than dining") rattled out

Ultimately Oxford failed him – he came down without a degree, and ironically, his downfall was a compulsory examination in Holy Scripture. But in Betjeman country Oxford assumes the proportions of some droll spa, Georgian in its refinement, Victorian in its changing pattern, Edwardian in its indulgence. He went there to take its waters, his stay was full of the mood of holiday. Years afterwards, it supplied him with a gallery of kindred and, in recollection, a haven of elegance and sophistication.

Long roads hedged and shrubbed, always to Woodstock or Banbury, glimpses of Fisoned green through wrought-iron gates, little Chaucceresque faces on the gargoyled eaves and cornices, in the lanes at dusk bicycles swishing past suddenly, sounds of small rivers and distant choirs, across a court, a cello or madrigal from an upstairs window, languid bustle of student chatter in pubs, draped stripes of scarves, badges of ease – Oxford, the freewheeling lyceum of Betjeman country. The colleges are built in a cinnamon-coloured stone which borrows the light from the sun and pays it back to the twilight.

University was Betjeman's encore to Oxford. In 1917 he had left Highgate Junior School to attend, before Marlborough, the Dragon School in Oxford, taught by Gerald Haynes of shambling height, of cigarette on lower lip, of seminal and lifelong influence.

Wallflowers upon the ruined city wall,
Wistaria-mantled buildings in St. John's –
All that was crumbling, picturesque and quaint
Informed my taste and sent me biking off,
Escaped from games, for Architecture bound.

Magdalen College awaits you at the end of High Street: descend from Broad Street via Turf Street, past Lincoln College where John Wesley lived, past Brasenose, named for a brass-nosed door knocker, past the twin towers of All Souls upon whose

common-room door a man once hung upside down for ten seconds by the grip of his toes and collected his wager, past The Queen's College – oh! that wonderful library! – to aloof Magdalen, pronounced Maudlin.

The Cherwell flows under Magdalen Bridge. Longwall Street, which means what it says, is the other boundary. At the rear the swathes of the deer park broaden upwards to St. Cross Road. Gardens, meadows, parkland, one hundred acres of serenity, Magdalen's peace is secure. The college, founded in 1458 by William of Waynflete, Bishop of Winchester, sustains philosophy, theology and a fine choir. Along the buttresses – Betjemanesque boon – strut carved figures, a hippopotamus, a panther, a pelican. A real emu once resided – he died because the students fed him too much currant cake.

In honoured Magdalen memory, Betjeman is mentioned in the same breath as Oscar Wilde, who roomed with fans and blue china in the college's New Buildings. A *viva voce* examiner attempted to trap Oscar by hurling at him Chapter 27, the most difficult of the Acts of the Apostles, St. Paul's shipwreck, all nautical terminology. Wilde translated impeccably from the Greek. The foxed examiner shouted stop. Oscar begged to go on: "I *do* want to see what happened next . . ." And brawn – he routed by fist and boot four students who came to rag him in his room. (Ditto some years later; the miners in a Wild West boom town failed to appreciate his slim verse, or his green velvet suit with matching carnation. One belching drinker hopped a beer mug off Wilde's head – Oscar descended, beat the bejasus out of him, was chaired from the saloon triumphant.) But at Magdalen, brilliant though he was, they did not offer him a fellowship. "I'll be a poet," he cried. "I'll be a writer, a dramatist. Somehow or other I'll be famous, and if not famous, I'll be notorious."

Was it here too, on Magdalen Bridge, that Betjeman lay down in the street? A small crowd gathered. He rose, dusted himself down and walked away murmuring innocently: "I wondered what might happen!"

> My walls were painted Bursar's apple-green;
> My wide-sashed windows looked across the grass
> To tower and hall and lines of pinnacles.
> The wind among the elms, the echoing stairs,
> The quarters, chimed across the quiet quad
> From Magdalen tower and neighbouring turret-clocks,
> Gave eighteenth-century splendour to my state.

Each year, at six o'clock on May Day morning, the choir gathers in Magdalen tower. Punts slide in, a little silent vigil. And over the spires and the mellow roof-tops the notes of the choir float unfettered across the dawn, and then, the greater pealing, booming notes; the bells were installed by James I who called the tower of Magdalen "the most absolute building in Oxford".

Enter Magdalen into a small, grass-triangled, creamstone court, buttressed and pinnacled. In the dainty high chapel prayers are implored for the brass-remembered regiments. The warm country accent of the verger advises visitors towards Evensong. Organ music, a voluntary, like a judge's arrival, initiates the occasion, a hymn is tactfully declared, the air fills with gold shards of boy soprano sound. Is disbelief always suspended by the conjunction of such graces?

Outside, the cream cloisters are in shadow, the daylight is over, footsteps, or an occasional cheery hail, mutedly resound, the windows turn on their lights.

> A multiplicity of bells,
>   A changing cadence, rich and deep
> Swung from those pinnacles on high
> To fill the trees and flood the sky
>   And rock the sailing clouds to sleep.

Through a doorway, a don and two students hurry with their words, young and older, anxious and benign, the querying and the resolving; earnestness hangs behind them, pipesmoke in the air. The deer park opens out like the pages of an old album. Was John Betjeman one of the students who made the stags drunk on sugar lumps steeped in port?

The trees are smaller than their history. Not one would now hold 256 horses, or 3,456 men in its shade, as the Magdalen Oak did. In 1752, Edward Gibbon glimpsed a personal decline and fall in Magdalen – the year he spent in the college was "the most idle and unprofitable of my life" – and was sent down. Ivor Novello sang in the choir; Martin Routh, a centenarian president (for sixty-three years until 1854), refused to recognise the existence of the railways and offered as his quintessential advice, "always verify your references". Magdalen Bridge, says the porter on the way out, has been crossed by more bicycles than any bridge in history.

Is it possible to enumerate the colleges of Oxford? Thirty-something? Old porters will argue heatedly with you. Toss in some new names, twentieth-century colleges? "Not colleges at all, sir."

Hitler had reserved Oxford as his capital when he had conquered England. Cromwell stole the organ from Magdalen. Keats said that the Thames at Oxford had byways and backwaters "more in number than your eyelashes". Jan Morris dedicated one of her books, "*Gratefully To The Warden And Fellows Of St. Antony's College Oxford – except one*". And John Betjeman luxuriated in the privacy and pursuits, so rich after his Marlborough straits.

> Silk-dressing-gowned, to Sunday-morning bells,
> Long after breakfast had been cleared in Hall,
> I wandered to my lavender-scented bath;
> Then, with a loosely knotted shantung tie
> And hair well soaked in Delhez' Genêt d'Or,
> Strolled to the Eastgate. Oxford marmalade
> And a thin volume by Lowes Dickinson . . .

Betjeman the undergraduate aligned himself spiritually with the "aesthetes": "hearties" signified physique – bullying connotations. Parodies, intellectual games, arguments and epigrams supplied education at parties rather than examinations. Companions evolved into friends, loved, or – sadly, as with Basil, Marquess of Dufferin and Ava – commemorated.

> Friend of my youth, you are dead!
>   and the long peal pours from the steeple
> Over this sunlit quad
>   in our University city
> And soaks in Headington stone.

Girls were the mythologised Myfanwy, a latter-day Peggy Purey-Cust, clean-cut and willowy as Joan Hunter Dunn, lissom as Greta Hellstrom, the heroines he had yet to meet.

> Shall we ever, my staunch Myfanwy,
>> Bicycle down to North Parade?
> Kant on the handle-bars, Marx in the saddlebag,
>> Light my touch on your shoulder-blade.

In the streets today, they all still wander, replicated from Betjeman. In Blackwell's bookshop, where he ran up a large debt for extra-curricular architectural tomes (discharged years later – in irony – by his father's estate), they walk, bright-eyed in their privilege, enthusiastically hunting the coveted "First". *The Oxford Handbook*, published by the Students' Union, advises newcomers on the subject: "On arrival in Oxford you will soon find out about gnomes, those people who lock themselves away in the library for years in the hope of emerging with that most glittering of prizes – a First. Your Tutors will probably want you to become one. Don't listen. It is inevitable that Finals and their results, being such a common conversation-piece with some tutors and all friends, should be of some interest – but only muddled thinking produces an attitude of slavery to classified results and the myth of the Unattainable First." In which case, John Betjeman's thinking was certainly not muddled.

> Failed in Divinity! O, towers and spires!
> Could no one help? Was nothing to be done?
> No. No one. Nothing. Mercilessly calm,
> The Cherwell carried under Magdalen Bridge
> Its leisured puntfuls of the fortunate
> Who next term and the next would still come back.
> Could no one help? I'd seen myself a don,
> Reading old poets in the library,
> Attending chapel in an M.A. gown,
> And sipping vintage port by candlelight.

*   *   *

Oxford today is Betjeman-haunted. In the chapel at Magdalen, hearing the waterlike purity of the unbroken voices, taking tea in the Randolph Hotel, flirting with the variegated cakes on the trolleys, being inspected by the heads outside the Sheldonian Theatre, hearing Great Tom, the bell of Christ Church, ring at five past nine each evening (not nine o'clock, Oxford is suspended five minutes west of the Greenwich meridian), gazing at those buttresses of Magdalen – carved griffin, panther, hyena and werewolf – and the dessicated and gowned dons in their libraried rooms, the female students on their bicycles, erotic in their intellect: John Betjeman's Oxford is a state of mind, an unheeding, eccentric wonderland. In 1938, even Oxford raised an eyebrow of enquiry at one of the oddest books it has spawned. *An Oxford University Chest by John Betjeman Comprising A Description of the Present State of the Town and University of Oxford With An Itinerary Arranged Alphabetically* is a

quirked and rococo gazetteer. Was it an affectionate reflection – or a lampoon? The book falls into seven parts: the Three Oxfords, Undergraduates, Dons, College Servants, the Approaches to Oxford, Architectural Tour, and Notes on Some Oxford Novels.

Of the Three Oxfords, first comes Christminster, the archetypal seat of learning in a country town, the place for which Thomas Hardy's Jude the Obscure yearned. Betjeman, too, idealised it, lamented its progression. "As fields become pasture, as barns decay, as farmers are ruined and taxed, as the horse gives place to the lorry, as the food is shaken out of the tin, as the co-ops flourish, and as the multiple stores distribute their free gifts, so Christminster the market town decays, and another, more sinister community takes its place."

This new settlement is called Motopolis. "Though the bells ring, you cannot hear them above the motor-bicycles and gearchanging. As for the drinking, it is more often cocoa than vintage port. If ever the victory between town and gown has been decided, it has been decided now. And the victory is with Motopolis."

Motopolis is the community housing of the internal combustion engines of the Morris cars. "To escapists, to arty people like the author of these pages, the internal combustion engine is, next to wireless, the most sinister modern invention . . . with its cargo of cads, it poisons the air, endangers the streets, deafens the ears and deadens the senses. That its most successful manifestation in England should be at Oxford, of all places, passes belief."

Betjeman's third Oxford was the University, epitomised by Encaenia, the robed and maced public procession of dedication which winds through the city on the ninth Wednesday of the Trinity term. "The last flutter of the Registrar's gown disappearing through a stone archway, the voices of the crowd around you raised to normal pitch after the awed exclamations of admiration at so many first-class brains under such a variety of medieval headgear, at divers lovely robes flaring against soft-toned walls – and you will be wondering whence this pageant wound and to what old building of those that tower about you is it bound."

And, as he himself did, undergraduates come in sets, the fast men, the rich men, the hearties, the aesthetes: "The artistic and literary gentleman is expected to take an interest in music. He generally has a gramophone and some Bach records, some of the more subtle dance records, and never Wagner. This is sometimes described as aesthetic, and until lately 'aesthetes' were easily recognisable for their long hair or odd clothes. With the

advent of left-wing politics into modern verse, the aesthete has slightly changed his appearance. He is a little scrubby-looking nowadays; his tie alone flames out."

Dons, individuality rampant, hail from a mythical college, the typical St. Ervan's: ". . . the old Professor of Palaeontology who bicycles down the Banbury Road once a week wearing a speckled straw hat and Evangelical clothes, in order to deliver his mythical lecture to a mythical audience but really to get a few things for his wife at Grimbly Hughes: Mr. Clack who keeps the Common Room accounts so accurately and whose neat writing and underlining in different coloured inks are so admirable an expression of his personality . . . Mr. Dandruff we see rarely nowadays, except at meal times. For the last seventeen years he has been engaged on his important book *Two Years of Richard II's Internal Policy* which I see announced by the *Clarendon Press*."

College servants were, still are, stewards and scouts. "A good scout can coax a man from greed or parsimony to an appreciation of modest comfort: he can over-awe a cocoa-drinking don: he can sum up a flashy bounder; he is, if he is a really good scout, something of a snob, not necessarily in a matter of titles, but in food, drink and good manners. He is a distinctly conservative person, considering his wages."

In Oxford John Betjeman grew up. High spirits, port, elaborate clothing, a talent to amuse, erotic expression ("I often think that I would like / To be the saddle of a bike" was written with other poets, W. H. Auden, Louis MacNeice) and developing passions – churches, architecture, beautiful things past – all gushed forth in a fountain. Occasional, fashionably pink politics, countryside adventures in Bugattis or bull-nosed Morris Minors, solitary worship – Oxford invigorated him.

He lived among the colleges, roomed briefly "with a man called, appropriately, Pinching", made forays into the suburbs.

Belbroughton Road is bonny, and pinkly bursts the spray
Of prunus and forsythia across the public way,
For a full spring-tide of blossom seethed and departed hence,
Leaving land-locked pools of jonquils by sunny garden fence.

Thirty-five years later he wrote in the *Daily Telegraph*: "Like most of the best things in England, Oxford hides its treasures . . . It is a place of crumbling stone walls and bells chiming the quarters, of old stained glass, carved urns and cupolas, gothic arches and niches. It is irreplaceable."

CHAPTER
FIVE
IRELAND

Bells are booming down the bohreens,
  White the mist along the grass.
Now the Julias, Maeves and Maureens
  Move between the fields to Mass.
Twisted trees of small green apple
Guard the decent whitewashed chapel . . .

John Betjeman lived happily in Ireland from 1941 to 1943, a disguised press attaché in the British Embassy – "I think I was a spy!!" He even learnt a smattering of Gaelic, and many a volume of his work has been autographed "Sean O'Betjeman". Even more absurdly, he was once the assassination target of a lurking IRA gunman. But the poet was away that day; when the gunman subsequently scanned the Englishman's verses he removed the name from the list.

"The fair city of Dublin with its noble Georgian squares of Guinness-washed brick, its grey, granite churches and public buildings and its smells of turf smoke and brewing . . . Belfast with its substantial monuments of Victorian prosperity . . . the sweet city of Cork with its many waters . . ." Betjeman and Ireland continued as they began – house-guest and genteel host.

In the poems, too, Betjeman's Ireland is lyrical and graceful.

> Lush Kildare of scented meadows,
> Roscommon, thin in ash-tree shadows,
> And Westmeath the lake-reflected,
> Spreading Leix the hill-protected,
> Kneeling all in silver haze . . .

Over a century before Betjeman's arrival in Dublin, the Catholics had been emancipated by O'Connell the Liberator; all over the country the new churches arose and the slow excuse-me dance of Protestantism and pain-free Catholicism began.

When the Insurrection of 1916 eventually led to the Anglo-Irish Treaty of 1921, the old order changed as surely – if a little more slowly – as it had in Prussia or as it later would in Germany and Italy. And Protestant ownership waned in the egalitarian Republic.

When Betjeman arrived in Dublin, the new state was twenty years old. He was just in time to record the old ways of the Protestants, and witness their passing, and, at the same time, perceive the emergent people.

Irish history, as ever, was immediate and available – a century provided gossip, a millennium conversation. And the euphony – even the names sang their own tunes.

In Betjeman country, Ireland is a lost domain, green and watered with mists, a lovely, lonely, woodcut of manses and avenues, of limestone houses, high fields and faraway flashing lakes, of ivied walls, Georgian mouldings, and gravel paths and woodland. The society in which he moved was Anglo-Irish, the remnants of the gentry whose fortunes at best swerved, at worst disappeared, as the risen people of the Republic advanced.

When he dwelt among the Irish Protestants (in Clondalkin, on the outskirts of Dublin, "You could get there by steam train") their long supremacy was over. Once the treaty of 1921 was signed thousands of them departed voluntarily and sadly; and some fled, burnt out of their estates in anti-colonial reprisal. The minority who stayed on became the "Five Per Cent", for whom Yeats, the poet and senator, thundered his famous plea: "We are no petty people". Over many the mildew of poverty spread. In their quiet houses behind high demesne walls, in their ways, their means, their numbers, their religion, they were diminished.

> Within that parsonage
> There is a personage
> Who owns a mortgage
>   On his Lordship's land,
> On his fine plantations,
> Well speculated,
> With groves of beeches
>   On either hand –

And when Betjeman minuted meetings during his residence in Dublin he dated paperwork, mischievously and sentimentally, according to the liturgical calendar.

> The small towns of Ireland by bards are neglected,
>   They stand there, all lonesome, on hilltop and plain.
> The Protestant glebe house by beech trees protected
>   Sits close to the gates of his Lordship's demesne.

John Betjeman's Ireland is a history and geography lesson. "You know you are coming to a town by the presence of a high stone wall, probably built in the famine to provide work. This is now overgrown with ivy, and gaps in it show remains of a landscaped park, still with a few tall beech trees . . . the distant house, with its weedy walled garden and reed-choked lake, is the shell of an Adam-style mansion burnt down in 'The Troubles' . . . at the top of the town, the wide main road is flanked by handsome, plain, Georgian houses. On one side is the Glebe House, where the Church of Ireland Rector lives. Opposite is a terrace, known as the Mall, with long gardens at the back where the agent for the estate, the solicitor, the doctor and the bank manager have adjacent houses." Old Irish saying – if you had a tune to that you could sing it.

> But where is his Lordship, who once in a phaeton
>   Drove out twixt his lodges and into the town?
> Oh his tragic misfortunes I will not dilate on;
>   His mansion's a ruin, his woods are cut down.

Near every market town, wrought-iron gates, curved limestone wall, pillared entrances rang out the old society, the Big House, the cut-stone cornices, the kitchen garden, the three-quarter-bred hunters. Accents were clipped – hopeful Oxbridge: children were schooled at St. Columba's, Rathfarnham, County Dublin, or Portora, Enniskillen, County Fermanagh, finished at Trinity College.

The Army, or the Raj, or the plantations, tea and tobacco, offered places for those without seniority of inheritance. When the country changed hands in 1921, much dissolved, faded away, in a mournful mist of memory and forgotten estate.

> His impoverished descendant is dwelling in Ealing,
>   His daughters must type for their bread and their board,
> O'er the graves of his forebears the nettle is stealing
>   And few will remember the sad Irish Lord.

John Betjeman's disconsolation was not isolated. One of the more eminent Catholic men of letters, Sean O'Faolain, also worried then about babies and bathwater. That vivid strand of contribution, Burke, Swift, Yeats, was frailer, and no longer pulled the same influence. Upon many of the Protestants who stayed, genuine fear attended, afraid to venture opinions, unwilling to make any stand upon ground which was shifting.

The most obvious losers were the eccentric and egregious Anglo-Irish peerage. This curious breed entertained brilliance, idiosyncracy, superstition, humanitarianism or, often, plain madness.

As he encountered them, and as they had been, they were ripe for Betjeman's sense of satire. Even at the age of twenty-two he created Lord Mount Prospect, a mythical but wholly typical Irish peer. "Whenever I sit down to my solitary meal of an evening," Betjeman began, "I am put in mind of the many obscure Irish peers who are sitting down to theirs. Some, perhaps, in a room over the stables, gaze at the moonlit ruins of what was once a stately mansion; others sip port as the Adam decoration peels off the ceiling and falls with an accustomed thud to the floor. The wind sighs and sings through the lonely Irish night round the wet walls of every house and down each grass-grown drive until it causes even the stable bell to tinkle, although the clock has long ago ceased to work."

Lord Mount Prospect, otherwise Archibald Standish Cospatrick Reeve, is an Ember Day Bryanite, that "obscure sect founded by William Bryan, a tailor of Paternoster Row, and William Reeve, a chandler in the city of Exeter . . . They believe in a bodily resurrection and the sleep of the soul. They declare that the sun is four miles from the earth . . ."

His friend, Lord Octagon, breeds electric eels with the intention of harnessing their energies to light his house. Another friend, Lord Santry, has translated "the libretto of all the Savoy operas into Latin hexameters."

> On his gateway olden
> Of plaster moulded
> And his splendid carriage way
>   To Castle Grand,
> (They've been aquatinted
> For a book that's printed
> And even wanted
>   In far England)

Despite impressions to the contrary John Betjeman has only written a handful of poems about Ireland, and of these the

THE CHURCH, KINSALE. 2260. W.L.

longest and the most extraordinary came courtesy of the Anglo-Irish peerage. "Sir John Piers", in five distinctive parts, is a tale of love, intrigue and fancy, set in the misty lakelands near the town of Mullingar, fifty miles west of Dublin. In the topographical saucer that is Ireland, water has lodged in the middle. Loughs shine – Gowna, Iron, Owel, Derravaragh, Sheelin, beads on a rosary; flat country, a mixture of bog and mottled limestone, curlews and thoroughbred horses.

Mullingar rejoices in cattle, wide streets, agribusiness; masted and prowed by a Catholic cathedral. Turn left by the Market House, take the T9, the road to Tullamore, for five miles, and on the right the blue gates marked 'B' part into Belvedere.

> Oh, gay lapped the waves on the shores of Lough Ennel
> And sweet smelt the breeze 'mid the garlic and fennel,
> And sweeter and gayer than either of these
> Were the songs of the birds in Lord Belvedere's trees.

With varied metre and much poetic licence, Betjeman tells a tale of seduction and its consequences. In the Country Library at Mullingar, in the *Annals of Westmeath, Ancient and Modern*, by James Woods, Betjeman found the following story:

> In 1807, Sir John Piers, the last of the name who resided in Tristernagh, and who was a gambler, duellist, and spend-thrift, was a schoolfellow of the patriot, Lord Cloncurry. Shortly after the marriage of that nobleman [i.e. Cloncurry], Piers, who shared his hospitality and even received pecuniary aid from him, made a diabolical wager to ruin for life the happiness of the wedded pair.

In Betjeman's poem the seduction occurred at a fabulous picnic at Belvedere Lodge on the shores of Lough Ennel, when all the gentry gathered at a beauty spot across the lake.

> The grotto is reached and the parties alight,
> The feast is spread out, and begob! what a sight,
> Pagodas of jelly in bowls of champagne,
> And a tower of blancmange from the Baron Kilmaine.

Belvedere was a shooting-lodge then, huntin' and fishin' too. Peacocks decorate the grounds now; the gap-toothed ruin to the far left as you face the lake is the Jealous Wall – allegedly erected to restrain an earlier straying wife.

In 1806, Eliza Georgina Morgan, the young wife of Valentine

Lawless, the second Earl of Cloncurry, was nineteen. A small lady, two children, and she had a head that could be turned – although her husband's biographer, a hypocritical bigot called W. J. Fitzpatrick, wrote: ". . . A more unlikely person than Lady Cloncurry to prove unfaithful to him she had vowed to love, honour and obey, did not, perhaps, exist in Christendom. Can it be believed that such was the character which Sir John Piers resolved by every art of hell to wither and destroy?" John Betjeman did not share in Mr. Fitzpatrick's lugubrious opinions of Sir John Piers.

> Huzza for Sir John! and huzza for the fête,
> For without his assistance no fête is complete;
> Oh, gay is the garland the ladies will wreathe
> For the handsomest blade in the County Westmeath.

Sir John Bennet Piers was a descendant of one of Queen Elizabeth's soldiers, who was given Tristernagh nearby, and its land and abbey, in 1566. John became the sixth Baronet in 1798 at the age of twenty-six, married the daughter of a clergyman from neighbouring County Cavan, but she died, and he overcame his grief in a most gregarious fashion, which is how he received his reputation as a ladies' man.

He met Lady Cloncurry in 1806, at dinner in her home. Nothing untoward happened. A week later they met again. Shortly after that Sir John Piers began to write to her – letters which Mr. Fitzpatrick, the biographer, subsequently described as "composed in the common vulgar cant of the Circulating Library".

Lord Cloncurry described his wife as "innocent in her manners, pure in her mind and lovely in her person", and commissioned a marble replica of her size four foot. Which led Mr. Fitzpatrick to declare later: "Never were two persons united who appeared more happy or contented with their lot; the conduct of Lady Cloncurry was exemplary." But somehow, in all her exemplary, dainty-footed innocence, Lady Cloncurry forgot to tell her husband about the panting of Sir John Piers.

> Press to your cheeks / my hand so hot and wasted,
>   Smooth with my fingers / the freckles of your frown,
> Take you my abbey, / it is yours for always,
>   I am so full of / love that I shall drown.

The Cloncurrys lived, not at Belvedere, but at Lyons House in Celbridge near Dublin, on a colonnaded, watered, obelisked estate, hung with great artistic treasures, and now a research farm for the Department of Agriculture.

One day, when Cloncurry was out walking his lands at Lyons, Piers called again and found Lady Cloncurry alone in the drawing-room. Gaspar Gabrielli, a famous Italian painter of murals, was employed by Cloncurry at the time. On that fateful day he was, like Titian's model, perched on a ladder. "I was there in an angle of the room, painting the ceiling in the billiard-room which is next to the drawing-room, in which Lady Cloncurry sat. Sir John opened the door and looked inquisitively into the room, then he shut the door again and put down the little thing that stops the key-hole . . ." Quite. Gabrielli's wife was Lady Cloncurry's maid and on many occasions she had wondered to her husband about the dishevelled state of My Lady's clothing. Furthermore, she observed that Lady Cloncurry possessed a locket containing a miniature of Sir John Piers plus a lock of his hair.

In time her conscience assailed Lady Cloncurry and one night, while Piers was their house-guest, in the candle-lit deeps of her boudoir she threw herself at her husband's feet and on his mercy. According to Mr. Fitzpatrick: "Although the hour was only half-past-four, Lord Cloncurry rushed like a maniac from his chambers to that occupied by Sir J- P-. He thundered at the door, entered the room but found it empty." A fowling piece, which usually remained behind the door was gone, too. Quivering, Cloncurry descended the stairs. Aided by the dawn of a grey summer morning he searched the thickly wooded demesne of Lyons.

"At length in a retired part of the grounds Sir J- P- rose before him. Ere Lord Cloncurry gave expression to his feelings, he procured with admirable presence of mind the fowling piece from Sir J- P-, lest the hot and ungovernable temper of his false friend should lead him, in a moment of revengeful impulse, to discharge it."

Piers, with equally admirable presence of mind, fled – to the Isle of Man. The biographer summed up: "Rejoice, ye fiends, and devils of darkness, for the eyes of the Lord of Lyons will soon be bathed in tears and his nuptial couch hung in mourning."

In Ireland there was a law (only repealed a few years ago) which went under the name of Criminal Conversation, or Crim. Con, the statute by which an aggrieved husband could sue his wife's seducer – wives did not have similar redress. The sensational case of *Cloncurry v. Piers* opened on the 19th of February 1807 in the Court of King's Bench, Dublin. The courtroom was packed for each session and two separate publishers in the city issued booklets of each full day's proceedings which sold out as soon as they appeared. But – *Hamlet* without the Prince – Piers would not come back from the Isle of Man, nor could he be fetched (it was a civil action) from his exile.

> Alone with his thoughts when the wild waves are beating
> He walks round to Jurby along the wet sand,
> And there, where the moon shows the waves are retreating,
> He too would retreat to his own native land.

Cloncurry won the action phenomenally: twenty thousand pounds' damages. When Piers did return, he was ruined and all his lands in County Westmeath became the possessions of Cloncurry, with the exception of a high-walled cottage plot.

> My speculated avenues are wasted,
> The artificial lake is choked and dry,
> My old delight by other lips is tasted,
> Now I can only build my walls and die.

> I'll nail the southern wall with Irish peaches,
> Portloman cuttings warmed in silver suns,
> And eastwards to Lough Iron's reedy reaches
> I'll build against the vista and the duns.

Piers became known locally as the "Sabbath Man", appearing only on Sundays, a day on which civil debts could not be collected. Part of the folklore claimed that he died in a fall from one of his high walls, escaping from his do-it-yourself debtors' prison. But, in truth, he slipped away to Canada, married a Miss King and ripened gracefully.

Lady Cloncurry was cast out, disgraced by the court proceedings, disowned by her husband. She left Ireland, forfeited her title and her two children, and in time remarried, virtuously, a clergyman from Somerset, amid considerable anonymity.

Lyons House, with its Gabrielli murals, survives – as did Cloncurry, aggrieved but wealthier.

There is a footnote – albeit not one recorded either in the *Annals of Westmeath* nor by Fitzpatrick the biographer. It was alleged in the courtroom that Sir John Piers seduced Lady Cloncurry in the interests of a wager. No documentation was adduced to support the claim and Piers himself was absent. But local knowledge swore that the other party in the wager was Cloncurry himself.

*   *   *

Betjeman originally published "Sir John Piers" under a pseudo-nym "Epsilon" in the *Westmeath Examiner* in 1938. He was only thirty-two but in Ireland he had already found many of the in-gredients which were to hallmark his work. In "Sir John Piers" he wrote parody, amatory verse, mock-heroics, and made social and topographical comment, as well as satirising the Anglo-Irish peerage – and all done in a variety of metre.

The fusion of Betjeman and Ireland is profoundly satisfying – rich and still and deep: in Ireland he made poems from given situations, and he perceived too, where poems lie concealed, in moments or circumstances.

In "Ireland with Emily" he fathomed with a singular sensiti-vity the tribal sensibilities of Sunday morning mass. For gene-rations this weekly ritual, the drone of the prayers, the shuffled silence, the brown wood, the tall coloured windows, the cloth-of-gold priest, the fugue of the morning, has sustained the people.

> Gilded gates and doorways grained
> Pointed windows richly stained
> With many-coloured Munich glass.
>
> See the black-shawled congregations
> On the broidered vestment gaze
> Murmur past the painted stations
> As Thy Sacred Heart displays.

But "Ireland with Emily" is a lament too, a keening for the memory of that old society which built the Big Houses. On the overgrown estate today, rusted gates are propped up, or wired in place by the farmer whose animals graze the parkland.

> Sheepswool, straw and droppings cover,
> Graves of spinster, rake and lover,
> Whose fantastic mausoleum
> Sings its own seablown Te Deum,
> In and out the slipping slates.

How could an Englishman, of Marlborough and Magdalen, rubbed with class, rubied with Anglicanism – how could such an Englishman have become so aware of both the worm and the bud in Ireland? Others before him were content with topo-graphical description. In County Cork, Carlyle wrote about "desolate, bare, moory country; hanging now in clear wet; much bog, mainly bog; treeless and swept over by a harsh moist wind . . ." Across Connemara Thackeray described the "huge dark mountains in their accustomed livery of purple and green,

AT CLONMACNOISE. 2254. W L

a dull sky above them, and estuary silver bright below ... a pair of seagulls undulating with the waves over the water, a pair of curlews wheeling overhead ..." By Killarney Tennyson immortalised the splendour falling on castle walls and tuned the horns of elfland.

Betjeman drew together the land and the wet skies and the loneliness and the social antiquity and made love-poems for, and in, Ireland, and each ruined gate past which you drive becomes his symbol of something loved and lost.

> There is no one now to wonder
> What eccentric sits in state
> While the beech trees rock and thunder
> Round his gate-lodge and his gate.
> Gone – the ornamental plaster,
> Gone – the overgrown demesne
> And the car goes fast, and faster,
> From Dungarvan in the rain.

But through all the remembrances and wistfulnesses John Betjeman listened carefully, too, to the new Ireland. And music came of it. In his metre he recalled the ancient balladmakers and their broadsheets, the people of the land come into their own. The rhythms of their speech, their song, were gifts to a poet, and their sense of fun and their names lay around, waiting to be used.

> Through the midlands of Ireland I journeyed by diesel
> And bright in the sun shone the emerald plain;
> Though loud sang the birds on the thorn-bush and teasel
> They could not be heard for the sound of the train.
>
> The roll of the railway made musing creative:
> I thought of the colleen I soon was to see
> With her wiry black hair and grey eyes of the native,
> Sweet Moira McCavendish, acushla machree.

And the topography of his ballads was small and soft, too. His introduction to "The Small Towns of Ireland" begins: "Public houses in Irish country towns are very often general merchants as well. You drink at a counter with bacon on it. Brooms and plastic dustpans hang from the ceiling. Loaves of new bread are stacked on top of fuse wire and, over all, there is a deep, delicious silence that can be found only in Ireland, in the midlands of Ireland in particular – the least tourionsted and profoundest part of that whole sad, beautiful country." In the tones of the people this visiting balladmaker found his own tunes.

> I hear it once more, the soft sound of those voices,
>   When fair day is filling with farmers the Square,
> And the heart in my bosom delights and rejoices
>   To think of the dealing and drinking done there.

John Betjeman's Ireland is, finally, an evolved place. Once it was a large painting in oils, damaged by damp, an encrusted frame, hanging baronially over a mantel.

Now it is a poster on a town wall among the "colour-washed three-storey houses . . . tethered ass-carts and betting shops, and a 1916 monument in the middle of the square." It could be any town, Mitchelstown, Ferns, Castlebar, Mountrath. On the outskirts linger the remains of the old demesne, ruined, overgrown.

RIVER LAGAN. BELFAST. 2232. W. L.

In the centre, cut-stone courthouses with notices in Gaelic, peeling hotels, assured bastions of Catholic churches.

O my small town of Ireland, the raindrops caress you,
   The sun sparkles bright on your field and your Square
As here on your bridge I salute you and bless you,
   Your murmuring waters and turf-scented air.

PART TWO

CHAPTER
SIX
LONDON

Oh when my love, my darling,
   You've left me here alone,
I'll walk the streets of London
   Which once seemed all our own.

The vast suburban churches
   Together we have found:
The ones which smelt of gaslight
   The ones in incense drown'd;
I'll use them now for praying in
   And not for looking round.

John Betjeman's London echoes with an unanticipated loneliness. Traditional, empirical, homely, huge, gilded and carved and stuccoed – his London is all of these things but his verses about London sigh with hints and memories of disappointments, old hurts and the humdrumming sadness of everyday life.

A traveller in London will find the *Collected Poems* a rich and quirky gazetteer, and with it will fetch up in railway stations, ornate or unadorned, rows of terraced, frumpy streets, empires of reinforced concrete and glass, *fin-de-siècle* hotels and restaurants, embellished, fretworked iron bridges, slightly crazy churches, pillars and fountainheads of establishment and antique boroughs redolent of Georgian, Victorian and Edwardian rectitude – John Betjeman is an adventurous, offbeat and yet comforting guide to London.

And he knows his London, too. Byways, laneways, tributaries, plaques, statues, jags of skyline fill his poems, turn them into a Victorian cyclorama. And he freshens his capital with his view: in the section marked "London" his feather more than pulls its weight on the library scales. Consolingly he makes London more accessible. If a city must be "she", just as Rome is a goddess and Dublin is a whore/mother, so London is a lady – in whatever context you wish to use the word. And Betjeman's portrayal of her reflects the ideal relationship – physical, intellectual, spiritual.

*   *   *

During school holidays the young John Betjeman, unwillingly a migrant to Chelsea, still homesick for his beloved Highgate, determined – with friends – to explore London physically on his beloved trains.

> Great was our joy, Ronald Hughes Wright's and mine,
> To travel by the Underground all day
> Between the rush hours, so that very soon
> There was no station, north to Finsbury Park,
> To Barking eastwards, Clapham Common south,
> No temporary platform in the west
> Among the Actons and the Ealings, where
> We had not once alighted.

The tube was still a novelty. London's first Underground was opened less than a generation before John Betjeman was born: the City and South London Railway, from King William Street, via Elephant and Castle, and Kennington, to Stockwell, in its two tubes, one over the other, on 18th December, 1890. Eleven and a half miles per hour to begin with, and the passengers, ninety-six of them in three long carriages, sat in electrically lit, upholstered comfort. The windows were high and narrow on each side – the compartments were nicknamed "padded cells".

> We knew the different railways by their smells.
> The City and South reeked like a changing-room;
> Its orange engines and old rolling-stock,
> Its narrow platforms, undulating tracks,
> Seemed even then historic.

But the City and South London, independently owned, did not make a profit and in late 1912 it was taken over by a rival conglomerate, re-engineered, and exists now as a stretch of the irritating, self-bisecting Northern Line.

> Next in age,
> The Central London, with its cut-glass shades
> On draughty stations, had an ozone smell –
> Not seaweed-scented ozone from the sea
> But something chemical from Birmingham.

The Central London was inaugurated by the Prince of Wales on 27th June, 1900 (in the amused presence of a visiting American, Mark Twain) and it cost five times more – at three and three-quarter millions – than the City and South London. The Central London's two tunnels ran side by side from the Bank of England, via Chancery Lane, Tottenham Court Road, Oxford Circus, Bond Street, Marble Arch, Notting Hill Gate and Holland Park, to Shepherd's Bush. The tracks into the stations climbed upward to help the train slow down, the way outward ran down a gentle slope to help get up speed – which peaked at twenty miles per hour.

The Central London, too, yielded to greater commerce, and in the multiplicity of deals which characterised the early days of London's transport – whose history is as confusing as a map of the underground – it was taken over.

The second, the intellectual phase, in young's Betjeman's assimilation of his native territory also became a lifelong infatuation.

> Once on a stall in Farringdon Road I found
> An atlas folio of great lithographs,
> *Views of Ionian Isles*, flyleaf inscribed
> By Edward Lear – and bought it for a bob.
> Perhaps one day I'll find a "first" of Keats,
> Wedged between Goldsmith and *The Law of Torts*;
> Perhaps – but that was not the reason why
> Untidy bookshops gave me such delight.
> It was the smell of books, the plates in them,
> Tooled leather, marbled paper, gilded edge . . .

At least one part of young John Betjeman's London has not changed. Try the bookshops today for, say, a first edition of Joyce's *Ulysses* and be enthralled instead by *Critical and Historical Essays* contributed to *The Edinburgh Review* by Lord Macaulay, in three volumes; Longman, Green, Longman, Roberts & Green, with marbled edges, a ledger of learning; or *For Love of the King, A Burmese Masque* by Oscar Wilde, Methuen & Co. 1922. *This Edition on handmade paper is limited to 1000 copies*, originally costing eight and sixpence.

Memoirs of film stars from the 1950s, schoolboy annuals, *Eagle, Beano, Dandy*, collectors' items now, forests of *National Geographic* and *Reader's Digest*, year-books, old county guides, parish histories, expensive, engraved art books or books of photographs hailed thirty years ago as "innovative", now unremarkably timeless, anybody's memories, intimate first-person accounts of life with the Beatles, moody and large-format studies of nude Greek sculpture – these bookshops take prisoners, hold them incommunicado for hours.

> Forgotten poets, parsons with a taste
> For picturesque descriptions of a hill
> Or ruin in the parish, pleased me much;
> But steel engravings pleased me most of all –
> Volumes of London views or Liverpool,
> Or Edinburgh, "The Athens of the North".

The third means by which young Betjeman came to know London was more profound. His family worshipped, a standard practice; participation in the community of church and parish became fundamental in his life. And the odd, corniced and crusted churches he discovered for himself revealed different truths.

> All silvery on frosty Sunday nights
> Were City steeples white against the stars.
> And narrowly the chasms wound between
> Italianate counting-houses, Roman banks,
> To this church and to that. Huge office-doors,
> Their granite thresholds worn by weekday feet
> (Now far away in slippered ease at Penge),
> Stood locked. St. Botolph this, St. Mary that
> Alone shone out resplendent in the dark.
> I used to stand by intersecting lanes
> Among the silent offices, and wait,
> Choosing which bell to follow:

The image of the small, plump Marlborough schoolboy, standing quietly by the railings in a chilly twilit evening, hushed, waiting for a bell to summon him, compels wonder. In the shadows he stood, or sat or knelt, already the observer, in some dim, oak-pewed, plasterworked church, watching a lone parishioner "with cherries nodding on a black straw hat", listening to the reedy wheezing of the organ, and London, and its trains, bookshops, churches, became him.

"Anyone with affection and imagination," John Betjeman advised his newspaper readers in 1960, "can see the real London. There are two ways of seeing it. One is to go to the top of a tall new block of flats or offices on a clear day and survey the landscape. The other is to drive about it on a Sunday morning when the streets are empty."

More effectively, pursue his poems: the long passages in *Summoned by Bells*, several of the *Collected Poems*, as many lines as London has lanes, and among them all a recognisable immediate London is to be found, sought out and embraced.

> From the geyser ventilators
> Autumn winds are blowing down
> On a thousand business women
> Having baths in Camden Town
>
> Waste pipes chuckle into runnels,
> Steam's escaping here and there,
> Morning trains through Camden cutting
> Shake the Crescent and the Square.

Four hundred years ago, when William Camden was surveying these islands for his *Britannia*, he had no cause to mention some undistinguished fields, a few copses and gathered cottages north of the Thames. Nor could this revered headmaster of Westminster School have anticipated that his name would become synonymous with business girls having baths, Irish immigration, seedy and doubtful streets. Indeed William Camden had nothing at all to do with Camden Town. A Lord Chancellor, Charles Pratt, lived near Chislehurst where, over a century beforehand, William Camden had died. Pratt was elevated to the peerage, and, out of admiration, chose as his title, "Camden". The new earl, a whig, encouraged private enterprise – and, therefore, speculative building. Pratt's Camden became an area of strong, fine housing.

Betjeman's Camden, and its crescents and squares, is a mixed bag. On one level, behind the well-kept or newly rescued

wrought-iron balconies and window-boxes, dwell the discreetly comfortable middle classes, enjoying practical access to the City and the West End, plus a little modest North London fashion.

But in the houses and flats where Dickens placed Bob Cratchit the struggle for respectability begins. Three decades ago Robert Colville wrote in *London and the Northern Reaches* (to be found under "Topography" or "London" in a Betjemanesque second-hand bookshop): "It could not be denied that in the minds of a great many people Camden Town is synonymous with squalor and with a certain degree of rough living, to which, however, more than a touch of glamour pertains." And Camden Council claims to spend more money on the welfare of its citizens than any comparable borough in Britain, while the police, at public meetings, have to answer for carrying arms on duty.

The skyline of Camden is coloured in brick: Florentine hints, Victorian-turreted schools, bomb replacement estates, the Camden of the bathing business women is a teeming region of take-aways and tiny shops. In 1973 five female art students began making jewellery in a dishevelled warehouse by the Camden Lock on the Regent's Canal and now two hundred stalls sell old knives, acetate gramophone records, pottery, mittens, home-made chocolate, art deco and art nouveau bric-à-brac, goat cheese. Trendy persons, all leg-warmers and liberal thinking, throng the Lock at weekends; a couple of doors away the Round House Theatre has been forced to close for lack of interest – and capital – and the local magazine thrust into your hand describes life on the poverty line with a mother of three: "I used to buy brown loaves but had to stop, partly because the children liked it so much they ate too much and partly because I couldn't slice it thinly enough. I buy fruit once a week and at tea-time cut an apple into tiny slices, decorate it with segments of half a satsuma and scatter a few raisins over the top. It looks pretty and they think it a great treat after their sandwich but it doesn't go far between three growing children. No drinks between meals – except water." Along the mixed streets, where blocks of flats or differing crescent façades adjust the bomb damage of World War Two, exist the people in Betjeman's ballad:

> And behind their frail partitions
> Business women lie and soak,
> Seeing through the draughty skylight
> Flying clouds and railway smoke.
>
> Rest you there, poor unbelov'd ones,
> Lap your loneliness in heat.
> All too soon the tiny breakfast,
> Trolley-bus and windy street!

John Betjeman's first expeditions took him across North London – by his father's side, toddling down to the family works in Islington, or on schoolboy adventures when the stations at Kentish Town, Gospel Oak, Tufnell Park became landmarks. North London contained the aunts, the visitors, the parental friends of childhood, the bridge-playing, brougham-borne callers whose speech was mysterious, full of seen-but-not-heard, grown-up confidences. And North London yielded stories, stained-glass fragments.

> The new lumber of a London-going dray,
> The still-new stucco on the London clay,
> Hot summer silence over Holloway.
>
> Dissenting chapels, tea-bowers, lovers' lairs,
> Neat new-built villas, ample Grecian squares,
> Remaining orchards ripening Windsor pears.
>
> Hot silence where the older mansions hide
> On Highgate Hill's thick elm-encrusted side,
> And Pancras, Hornsey, Islington divide.

When he was at Oxford his friend and mentor Maurice Bowra observed that "Betjeman has a mind of extraordinary originality; there is no one else remotely like him," and Lord Birkenhead, to whom the remark was addressed, used it to introduce Betjeman's *Collected Works*. In "An Incident in the Early Life of Ebenezer Jones, Poet, 1828" Betjeman plaited his narrative ability, his feeling for North London, his fear of bullying, his Dickensian sense of period.

Ebenezer Jones, minor poet, clerk, and Calvinist, attended a boys' academy at the foot of Highgate Hill, the Reverend John Bickerdike's school. On a hot summer day, when Ebenezer was eight, the Incident occurred from which Betjeman, assisted by secondhand browsing, unwound his poem.

> A lurcher dog, which draymen kick and pass
> Tongue lolling, thirsty over shadeless grass,
> Leapt up the playground ladder to the class.
>
> The godly usher left his godly seat,
> His skin was prickly in the ungodly heat,
> The dog lay panting at his godly feet.

The tension grew. The boys held their breath, afraid to look or murmur. Clearly the big, bull-necked usher intended to hurl the dog to the street far below.

"YOU SHALL NOT!" clear across to Highgate Hill
A boy's voice sounded. Creaking forms were still.
The cat jumped slowly from the window sill.

Little Ebby had left his desk, putting the older boys to shame
with his moral courage, challenged the tyrannical usher. John
Betjeman took his account of the occurrence from Ebenezer's
brother, Sumner Jones. "But even while the words passed his
lips, the heavy fall was heard, and the sound seemed to travel
through his listening form and face, as, with a strange look of
anguish in one so young, he stood still, threw up his arms, and
burst into an uncontrollable passion of tears." Even with poets,
by their actions you shall know – and immortalise – them.

Look on and jeer! Not Satan's thunder-quake
Can cause the mighty walls of Heaven to shake
As now they do, to hear a boy's heart break.

Be warned about North London. Do not always look for
grace and gracious mansions. The artisan territory of the Holloway Road is topographically squalid, uneven and shabby and
plain. Leaving Mr. Bickerdike's school behind, this long sweep
of North London, Holloway to Highbury, with its stingy,
stringy stretches of buildings, produces that sinking depression
born of inelegant service architecture, and overdue repairs. See
it in the winter rain, Stygian gloom: in the summer light, drab
and sooted, an unfragrant place to live, a good place to leave . . .

From Canonbury, Dalston and Mildmay Park
The old North London shoots in a train
To the long black platform, gaslit and dark,
On Highbury Station once and again.

Highbury and Islington Station has yellow doors, circles for
windows. Beneath the pigeons above the long, frugal over-
ground platform, grow weeds, unshaven tufts, in crevices over
bricked-out windows. The pillars came from some grown-up
building set, rounded, characterless, anonymous. Slashes of dia-
monds, brown, drab, ochre, buff, provide a decor in need of
an idea.
Highbury and Islington Station is a most versatile point of
departure; Canonbury, Hackney Central, Hackney Wick, Stratford, West Ham, Canning Town, Custom House, Silvertown,
North Woolwich where *are* all these places? – change at Stratford, watch it, Stratford low level – for Central Line (and Ilford,
Shenfield, Southend Victoria), Dalston Junction, Broad Street.

On the Up platform the timetable is a cornucopia, a parochial Cook's Tour: Caledonian Road, Primrose Hill, Finchley Road and Frognal, Willesden Junction, the Actons, Central and South, Gunnersbury, far away tempting Richmond, Harrow and Wealdstone, Hatch End . . . stop, stop! Exchange one exotic temptation for another – travel underground instead and meet the dowager queen of railway stations.

"In England, St. Pancras is less known as a Roman boy martyr than as a London railway station." John Betjeman did not joke when he wrote about trains and their trappings. "Even the former borough, and the old and new parish churches from which it took its name, are less in the public mind than that romantic cluster of towers and gables which still dominates King's Cross and district."

Look at it. The russet quarry colour, brick brocade, with its apostrophes and curlicues, renders wedding cakes austere. The innumerable niches and notches, *haut* folds in a *coutured* gown, reduce most nearby buildings to home dressmaking. This is

grandeur on parade, this is an oratorio of a building. From every angle, but particularly from the rear, St. Pancras is a château, a fairy castle, Hans Andersen, the Brothers Grimm.

You must be careful, though, to give credit where credit is due: for St. Pancras Station, read St. Pancras Hotel and Station. The station came first, two hundred and forty feet of rib-span, iron-cast, tie-beamed and glassed, finished by William Barlow, engineer, in 1868, the largest unsupported roof in the world. Over four years later, Sir George Gilbert Scott's architecture was unveiled to the public, as the Midland Hotel opened its doors to the businessmen who came in from Derby and elsewhere on the Midland Railway. Six hundred of them could stay at St. Pancras, in tremendous style, with hydraulic lifts, electric bells to the touch, lavish fireplaces in the rooms, a wonderful staircase, high and long.

St. Pancras blessed Victoriana at its greatest – Gothic and monied. The station was brilliantly designed to cope with fifty trains a day at platform level; and, beneath, at street level, thousands of barrels of beer from Burton-on-Trent. The hotel was libelled by the rumour that Gilbert Scott merely adjusted existing plans – those which Lord Palmerston had rejected for the Foreign Office a decade earlier. Ultimately the building was turned into offices in the 1930s, as tasteless and as functional as the food produced by the catering company which it houses. "More damage," cried the poet, "has been done to London and our other old towns by 'developers' and their tame architects than ever was done by German bombing. No one can object to the clearance of what is shoddy and badly built: St. Pancras Station and its hotel, now called Midland Chambers, are neither. It is horrible to contemplate such careful work being destroyed . . ."

St. Pancras has survived – just. Once, it even outstripped Highbury and Islington; St. Pancras had a national versatility. Now its responsibilities have been cut. But the ticket hall is wonderfully restored, embroidered with wood and plaster. On the short platforms passengers still line up for journeys to Derby, Nottingham, Sheffield. Alas, the hotel is silent. From the station look up and you will see little windows, dormered and secretive, maids' rooms, from which they could gaze down at the gentlemen with the "brass" coming to stay in the Midland Hotel at St. Pancras Station, bringing with them prospects of love and lucky marriage.

*   *   *

When the great bell
BOOMS over the Portland stone urn, and
From the carved cedar wood
Rises the odour of incense,
I SIT DOWN
In St. Botolph Bishopsgate Churchyard
And wait for the spirit of my grandfather
Toddling along from the Barbican.

The City of London has entranced John Betjeman since boyhood. Apart from the "Italianate counting-houses, Roman banks" and the little churches of his winter afternoons, the mood of the City mesmerised him too. More than once his prose has tried to come to terms with this two-thousand-year-old powerful, much churched, square mile citadel. In one breath he wrote, "The City of London is an English mystery. Behind its gold watch beats a warm heart, but under its silk hat is a shrewd head. The head and heart are often at war, and the former usually wins, hence the modern appearance of the City and its inhuman cliffs of rent-collecting slabs."

But in another breath the romance of the City had taken him over completely. "In the City on a still evening, sounds of glee-singing may be heard from lighted windows of livery company halls. Candles glitter on silver and gold plate; red robes trimmed with ermine are outlined against cedar wood: the light sparkles in vintage port and in the vast kitchens the caterers are packing away the remains of the venison."

And in yet another breath he scathed the people of the City:

> Business men with awkward hips
> And dirty jokes upon their lips,
> And large behinds and jingling chains,
> And riddled teeth and riddling brains,
> And plump white fingers made to curl
> Round some anaemic city girl,
> And so lend colour to the lives,
> And old suspicions of their wives.

From North London approach the City by one of the hills upon which it is built, Ludgate Hill, where they buried pre-Roman King Lud. And such names as you find coming down the Farringdon Road: Cowcross Street, animals bound for Smithfield Market; Snow Hill originally Snore Hill, named by late-night arrivals at a coaching inn; Turnagain Lane, because the River Fleet was not bridged here; Seacoal Lane, which is *why* it was not bridged – the coal barges docked within the City, along the Fleet. Here policemen wear different uniforms, no department stores, only sandwich bars, office stationery, pubs with extraordinary opening hours, beneath Sir Christopher Wren's citadel. Does St. Paul's guard the City's morals? And is that why it needed to be the largest cathedral in Christendom?

In AD 43 the Emperor Claudius decided to annex Britain – the Belgae were giving trouble and so were some of the native tribes. Forty thousand Roman soldiers, some of them German, crossed from Boulogne and eventually found themselves on the high gravelly bank of the River Walbrook, now called Cornhill. Was there earlier a Celtic watering place, "Llyn-Din", the Hill of the Pool – hence Londinium?

> Sunday Silence! with every street a dead street,
>   Alley and courtyard empty and cobbled mews,
> Till "tingle tang" the bell of St. Mildred's Bread Street
>   Summoned the sermon taster to high box pews.

And neighbouring towers and spirelets joined the ringing
    With answering echoes from heavy commercial walls
Till all were drowned as the sailing clouds went singing
    On the roaring flood of a twelve-voiced peal from Paul's.

Oh, can the inspiration for Betjeman's "Monody on the Death of Aldersgate Street Station" always have been so bland? Aldersgate, where is your ceremony now? You were once the means by which James I arrived from Scotland to claim England, you watched John Milton's literature commence here, and a plaque on a low Barbican wall commemorates the 24th of May 1738 when thirty-five-year-old John Wesley listened to a reading of a Martin Luther preface and saw the light.

Of which there is not much now in Aldersgate Street – a garage, some gun-grey cast concrete, shaled cliffs of tower blocks and buildings with gritted teeth in the Barbican. Visitors seeking permission to ascend to high balconies for the view are watched carefully lest they jump: are residents afforded the same courtesy? If necessary return to find St. Giles, Cripplegate, Lilliputian and red-bricked, hidden in among the feet of the giant Barbican towers; return, too, to St. Botolph's, the grass in its park is a boon; otherwise radiate back towards St. Paul's – Aldersgate Street, by the Ironmongers' Hall and the Barber Surgeons' Hall and once the main entrance to London from the North, does not merit revisiting.

Snow falls in the buffet of Aldersgate station,
    Toiling and doomed from Moorgate Street puffs the train,
For us of the steam and the gas-light, the lost generation,
    The new white cliffs of the City are built in vain.

Better to travel on to the next poem: walk, if you can bear the chrome claustrophobia, the journey affords oddities. The Bank of England does not immediately give the impression that its Secretary could have written, in 1908, *The Wind In The Willows*: correspondence from minor banks abroad, when the map of the world was so red, required to end "I remain, Sir, Your Obedient Servant", rebellious Irish bank clerks crossed out all but the "I". On a still, empty weekend, these streets are canyons offering occasional felicities – a tiny park fornenst St. Paul's, Carter Lane where Guy Fawkes met his plotters, Wardrobe Terrace where the royal robes were stored before the Great Fire of London and Addle Hill which could, should offer its name to this entire rabbit-warren neighbourhood.

"There are 25 bridges over the Thames between the Tower of London and Twickenham," counted John Betjeman. "Eight are of cast iron and carry railways. The remaining 17 are of varying materials – stone, cast iron and concrete, in that chronological order, and carry roads." Blackfriars Bridge replaced the earlier Pitt Bridge, named for a Prime Minister in 1760: but a bridge, too, is a long time in politics and, instead, the Dominican friars were commemorated in Joseph Cubitt's new bridge a century later.

Waterloo Bridge also replaced an earlier, more beautiful, bridge – of Cornish granite. "It was long and flat, with nine semi-elliptic arches, with coupled Doric columns between them," regretted John Betjeman, "and was considered by Canova to be the finest bridge in Europe. We, who remember it, can recall the perfect background it made to Somerset House, and distant views of the dome of St. Paul's. On the Embankment side some of its nobly simple granite detail survives. For not very convincing reasons about its safety and width, it was destroyed before the War . . ." But the new bridge retains the most absorbing, power-filled view, St. Paul's to the east, Westminster to the west, London clasped between Church and State.

> Let me take this other glove off
> As the *vox humana* swells,
> And the beauteous fields of Eden
> Bask beneath the Abbey bells,
> Here where England's statesmen lie,
> Listen to a lady's cry.

Why is John Betjeman ashamed of having written, would gladly disown, "In Westminster Abbey", dismisses it as "merely comic verse, and competent magazine writing, topical and tiresome"? Dwarfed by the building perhaps – as who must not be, and falling back upon sarcastic wit? (For much the same, if more elegant, reason, perhaps as the oaf who placed the empty whisky bottle upon the newly unveiled green stone slab for Dylan Thomas?)

NEW GOVERNMENT OFFICES   FOREIG

Gracious Lord, oh bomb the Germans.
Spare their women for Thy Sake,
And if that is not too easy
We will pardon Thy Mistake.
But, gracious Lord, whate'er shall be,
Don't let anyone bomb me.

One thing is certain: Betjeman's gloved lady will never utter her outlandish prayer so easily in Westminster Abbey again. Hordes of tourists, uncaring of the Lord, do not even whisper. Holding hands, arms and shoulders bare, legs in shorts, they clamber, ants in search of a photograph album. Flee them – rush past Poets' Corner, pause not to count the variety of architectural styles, blow a kiss to the tomb of Mary Queen of Scots. Ban the tourists, keep them out, free the Abbey once again, for true Betjeman natives.

Now I feel a little better,
What a treat to hear Thy Word,
Where the bones of leading statesmen,
Have so often been interr'd.
And now, dear Lord, I cannot wait
Because I have a luncheon date.

Outside in the sunlight, Whitehall shimmers impersonally. The mixed architectural styles, added on from half-century to half-century, give nothing away but uncaringness, imperviousness. The atmosphere wheezes power: democracy terminated, would Whitehall continue in perpetuity, offering rare human redress of its decisions? John Betjeman never displayed affection for Whitehall – respect certainly, admiration even, but never fondness. "Just as an old church is the history of its parish in terms of stone, so is Whitehall the embodiment of the history of England," he wrote carefully. "The weakness of this analogy is that whereas most churches are open for the public to inspect,

it is well-nigh impossible to see inside Whitehall. Buff passes and uniformed vergers guard the sanctuary." Even the smaller charms of Number 10, Downing Street seem contrived – such a street of similar proportions, in any other part of London, would cherish neighbours. But then, Number 10, Downing Street rarely needs to borrow a cup of sugar.

Check out the upper reaches of the 40th and 50th and 60th Streets in New York for Damon Runyon and Tom Wolfe; scout the villages of Paris and you will touch paragraphs of Georges Simenon; by street corners in Dublin expect to glimpse Swift or half blind O'Casey or rolling Behan or flowing Yeats. In London, here comes everybody. Dickens, supremely ubiquitous, and Trollope, and Dr. Johnson and Thackeray and Wordsworth on Westminster Bridge, and now, John Betjeman, too, paddling his way about the buildings, Norman Shaw this and Gilbert Scott that. Sometimes his eccentric sensibilities delighted in structures not strictly architectural. Friends tell the story of the poet, in his thirties, crossing a busy street during an immense traffic jam. Every vehicle had ground to a long and irritated halt, including a chauffeured Bentley in which sat a superior and chilly lady. She was wearing a spectacular hat and an expression of considerable annoyance. Betjeman startlingly rapped on the car. As the window slipped down a few noiseless and cautious inches and she raised an enquiring eyebrow, the poet merely had one comment: indicating her hat with a nod, he said, "I say – smart" and strolled away.

> He sipped at a weak hock and seltzer
> As he gazed at the London skies
> Through the Nottingham lace of the curtains
> Or was it his bees-winged eyes?
>
> To the right and before him Pont Street
> Did tower in her new built red,
> As hard as the morning gaslight,
> That shone on his unmade bed.

The Cadogan Hotel where Oscar Wilde was arrested in 1895 is a hotel for taking tea. No self-respecting building may be egregious on Sloane Street, nor would the Cadogan want to: other hotels elsewhere may indulge in that sort of thing. The gold letters over the creamy pillars say no more than they need to: the front hall accommodates a deep sofa and several Americans in mackintoshes. The wainscoting glows a gentle oaken colour, the corridors inside are dark and respectable and labyrinthine, the late Victorian and Edwardian incense lingers.

"More hock, Robbie – where is the seltzer?
Dear boy, pull again at the bell!
They are all little better than *cretins*,
Though this *is* the Cadogan Hotel."

Betjeman was still a young man, in his early thirties, when he wrote "The Arrest of Oscar Wilde at the Cadogan Hotel". Was Wilde guilty? The poet does not say, sits on the fence, even though they were both Magdalen men, with many aesthetic sympathies. When the poem was published it was greeted as a lark, a sort of pantomine for two voices.

A thump and a murmur of voices –
("Oh why must they make such a din?")
As the door of the bedroom swung open
And TWO PLAIN CLOTHES POLICEMEN came in:

"Mr. Woilde, we 'ave come for tew take yew
Where felons and criminals dwell:
We must ask yew tew leave with us quoietly
For this *is* the Cadogan Hotel."

Wonderfully, the Cadogan Hotel still makes the scene imaginable. Sit in a corner, order tea, overhear the quiet voices of the rich travellers, severe French, cultured American. Light, a weak sun, shafts across the floor from somewhere, through a high window. Chintz, superior quality, ambers and umbers, enveloping chairs, silent service, real linen. At any moment, the Roman Emperor carved from suet might sweep through in his coat with the velvet collar, the large lips, the high head, centre-parted hair, fat shoulders, effete stride: the hotel would stop breathing, no sound, an extra-loud clink of a cup somewhere . . .

He rose, and he put down *The Yellow Book*.
He staggered – and, terrible-eyed,
He brushed past the palms on the staircase
And was helped to a hansom outside.

*　　　*　　　*

Betjeman traverses London. For a time he lived in Cloth Fair, on the edge of the City, near the Smithfield Market, by lovely, dark-eyed, exclusive Charterhouse Square. During a temporary change in his arrangements he moved off down the river to Rotherhithe. "It struck me then that houses hanging over water are the ideal antidote to the noise and diesel fumes of modern

big cities . . . At low tide there would be the distant chug of a
passing tug and a few seconds later the swish of the waves caused
by her wake rippling over the pebbles and mud below my window. At high tide after a tug had passed the water made a plop-
ping sound right against my bedroom wall as though I were
in a ship's hold . . . I put my bed on the river side of the room
and it was delicious to go to sleep to the solacing sounds of
water . . ."

He fought battles for conservation, attacked the various London boroughs and their councils and their architects for crass-
ness in their destruction of the old in favour of less interesting
new. He recorded, year in, year out, the changing of the skyline,
for better but most often for worse, and he stayed in touch with
the people, watched them, touched them and was touched by
them, held them up like votive offerings in his verses.

The heavy mahogany door with its wrought-iron screen
    Shuts. And the sound is rich, sympathetic, discreet.
The sun still shines on this eighteenth-century scene
    With Edwardian faience adornments – Devonshire Street

No hope. And the X-ray photographs under his arm
    Confirm the message. His wife stands timidly by.
The opposite brick-built house looks lofty and calm
    Its chimneys steady against a mackerel sky.

When did he see them – late on a quiet Thursday afternoon, or a Tuesday, just before lunch? And in Devonshire Street? Not Harley Street round the corner? Devonshire Street, you see, cannot be called remarkable: even the faiences are dull in their glaze, brown rather than bright. Certainly the doors are discreet and rich, much-plated Mr. This and Mr. That, by appointment; not an ordinary street, nor an extraordinary street.

> No hope. And the iron nob of this palisade
> So cold to the touch, is luckier now than he
> "Oh merciless, hurrying Londoners! Why was I made?
> For the long and painful deathbed coming to me?"

London hurts, in or out of Betjeman. The arid bluster of the Holloway Road, the eyeless grandeur of Whitehall, the death of Aldersgate Street: but Betjeman's guidance eases the pain – in the little nooks of the real City, in the crannies of St. Pancras, in the tiny, condensation-filled bathrooms of Camden Town, he is a contented guide, despite the sadness.

> She puts her fingers in his as, loving and silly,
> At long-past Kensington dances she used to do
> "It's cheaper to take the tube to Piccadilly
> And then we can catch a nineteen or a twenty-two."

CHAPTER
SEVEN
KENT
AND
SURREY

Take me, Lieutenant, to that Surrey homestead!
  Red comes the winter and your rakish car,
Red among the hawthorns, redder than the hawberries
  And trails of old man's nuisance, and noisier far.
Far, far below me roll the Coulsdon woodlands,
  White down the valley curves the living rail,
Tall, tall, above me, olive spike the pinewoods,
  Olive against blue-black, moving in the gale.

South of London, in Kent and Surrey, lies the nirvana of Betjeman country, idealised and idealistic, brooched, twilled England. Politics rarely arise in Betjeman's poems – but guess how they vote in his nirvana?

> Deep down the drive go the cushioned rhododendrons,
>   Deep down, sand deep, drives the heather root,
> Deep the spliced timber barked around the summer-house,
>   Light lies the tennis-court, plantain underfoot.

Where is this land of lush valleys, where conifers and laurel protect the gardens and beam greenily down on the occupants, where half-timbered houses stand confident and private behind high hedges and long lawns, where the residents drink gin-and-tonic, Pimms, sherry, play eighteen holes once a week; where the shopping is bestowed on small well-behaved towns, and one knows one's butcher and one's butcher knows his place?

> When sunset gilds the Surrey pines
> The fam'ly usually dines.
> So later, in the Surrey dark,
> Make for Poonah Punkah Park,
> And by the monument to Clive
> You'll come to Enniscorthy Drive,
> Coolgreena is the last of all,
> And mind the terrier when you call.

To the traveller, the foreigner, gently exploring these discreet homelands, Surrey and Kent are deceptive. Misinterpret the signposting in the poems, and this grass-green corner, with its luxuriant foliage and restrained ways, will never yield its secrets; the natives, though they do it as discreetly as butlers, as smarmily as Cardinals, will sling you out! The clue, the key, to this Arcadia will be found in Betjeman's defence of himself, a half-line in the introduction to *Old Lights for New Chancels*: "I see no harm in trying to describe overbuilt Surrey in verse, but when I do I am not being satirical but topographical . . ."

Driving is quite convenient (although the trains are very good indeed). Unfortunately, the early part of the journey downward is, well, unprepossessing; still, if you look upward you will see, in Brixton, some perfectly lovely architecture, yes, perfectly lovely. Victorian mouldings and lintels and things. On Streatham High Road do not be misled geographically by a shop calling itself Che Guevara of Kensington – nor theologically by a church banner yelling "Come in for a Faith lift". Ally's Owl

Shop sells ice-skates – directly across from the sward of
Streatham Common, by which also grazes a company called
Cow Industrial Polymers. Soon you will be in Croydon, once
Surrey, now Greater London, and when John Betjeman was a
boy a place with those happy, mildly mysterious things, family
connections:

> In a house like that
>   Your Uncle Dick was born;
> Satchel on back he walked to Whitgift
>   Every weekday morn.

Archbishop Whitgift, obviously. He prayed with Queen
Elizabeth I on her deathbed, and he intended for Croydon "an
hospitall and abiding place for the finding, sustenation and relief
of certain maymed, poore, needie or impotent people to have
continuance forever". To find the Hospital of the Holy Trinity
– built in 1596 – you must steel yourself. As you drive past A.
& P. Stallion, Ltd., – wait for it – Turf Accountants, and enter
the town, put your aesthetic sensibilities away, face that awful
skyline with unfettered equanimity.

Who did it? Who permitted it? Betjeman, come and preach
here, set up a soap-box; in some countries where official concern

becomes grisly, they exhibit shattered, battered cars by the roadside to caution speeding motorists. Croydon should thus be the
exhibit for all reckless planning authorities.

Everywhere, high, graceless office blocks bully the little old
town. Uncouth government offices, obtuse insurance company
buildings – this is what John Betjeman fought: in print, in
broadcasts, his fiercest polemical outbursts were aimed at the
sort of planners who brought their bane to Croydon.

> All fields we'll turn to sports grounds, lit at night
> From concrete standards by fluorescent light:
> And over all the land, instead of trees,
> Clean poles and wire will whisper in the breeze.
> We'll keep one ancient village just to show
> What England once was when the times were slow –

And Archbishop Whitgift's hospitall, its dignity somehow in-
tact, shrinks by the corner of George Street, its values ignored.
Around it, echoes of the littler Croydon, the town's quiet Victorian strengths which the planners vandalised; over Grants,
directly across the street, the frieze casts its mind back: MILLI-
NERY RIBBONS LONDON HOUSE LACE GLOVES SILKS DRESSES
LONDON HOUSE MANTLES LINENS. Behind the hospital, beneath

the cowed Victorian commercial façades – "A.D. 1895" – The Sun Dance Centre Health Studio vies with the seafood restaurant called Hook, Line and Sinker, sacred and profane. The towers at the end of the street look down with the sort of security offered by a private army of uniformed thugs; and it is difficult to believe that Croydon was once a town in Surrey.

> Boys together in Coulsdon woodlands,
>   Bramble-berried and steep,
> He and his pals would look for spadgers
>   Hidden deep.
>
> The laurels are speckled in Marchmont Avenue
>   Just as they were before,
> But the steps are dusty that still lead up to
>   Your Uncle Dick's front door.

Put Croydon behind you! Drive out, into the countryside, to Purley, to Kenley, rolling wooded countryside. If you must, take the M25 towards Sevenoaks; if you do, you will miss Westerham and Churchill's Chartwell. But the road to Betjeman country winds off down through the woods, Sevenoaks in the east, Chiddingstone to the west, and ahead, Betjeman's "Eunice", of Royal Tunbridge Wells.

> With her latest roses happily encumbered
>   Tunbridge Wells Central takes her from the night,
> Sweet second bloomings frost has faintly umbered
>   And some double dahlias waxy red and white.
>
> Shut again till April stands her little hutment
>   Peeping over daisies Michaelmas and mauve,
> Lock'd is the Elsan in its brick abutment
>   Lock'd the little pantry, dead the little stove.

This is a long town. From Tunbridge Wells Central Eunice could also catch trains to wild Eridge and exotic Uckfield.

> I can see her waiting on this chilly Sunday
>   For the five-forty (twenty minutes late),
> One of many hundreds to dread the coming Monday
>   To fight with influenza and battle with her weight.
>
> Tweed coat and skirt that with such anticipation
>   On a merry spring time a friend had trimm'd with fur,
> Now the friend is married and, oh desolation,
>   Married to the man who might have married *her*.

Tunbridge Wells glows in a maidenly way, a settled lady of some years who has not sold out to a vulgar husband – as Croydon has. Henrietta Maria, the Queen of Charles I, recuperated here from the birth of Charles II, but it was Edward VII who made plain Tunbridge Wells "Royal". The chalybeate waters still flow, at the end of the Pantiles, a long colonnade, hints of Jacobethan. This could be a whaling street in New England, clapboarded and white and tiles and bow windows.

An air of precision hangs over this spa town. Where Bath wears flounced gowns Tunbridge Wells prefers pleated skirts. This atmosphere of the particular bred the Fowlers, Henry Watson Fowler and Frank George Fowler, of the *Dictionary of Modern English Usage*. Jane Austen's father taught a few miles away at Tonbridge, Thackeray spent school holidays here, Tennyson brought his mother to take the waters, A. A. Milne did his shopping here even as he was building *The House at Pooh Corner*; Daniel Defoe said, "Company and diversion is the main business of the place and those people who have nothing to do anywhere else seem to be the only people who have anything to do at Tunbridge."

And John Betjeman's frail Eunice leaves Tunbridge Wells Central on the Sunday five-forty back to London.

Home's here in Kent and how many morning coffees
   And hurried little lunch hours of planning will be spent
Through the busy months of typing in the office
   Until the days are warm enough to take her back to Kent.

*   *   *

Among poets, ancient and modern, John Betjeman is troublesome. By harsh literary rights should he not be a songwriter in his beloved music halls? His poems carry a two-edged sword. His subjects are "popular" – his treatment of them popularly expressed. Lord Birkenhead's introduction to the *Collected Poems* pinned the point: "This sense of place, so varied and so tender, has led Betjeman into a calculated risk, that of being typed as the poet of the suburbs, and many have wrongly assumed this addiction to be either a pose or a hoax on the public, and yet another example of that double-bluff humour in which his somewhat perverse mind undoubtedly delights . . ." But what other poet deliberately or accidentally, satirically or topographically, has conjured with the kind of landscape which flows past the window on the roads from Tunbridge Wells in Kent across to East Grinstead in West Sussex up to Reigate, in warmest Surrey? The very names, on the houses and roadside

halts, support Betjeman's argument that he does not wish to interrogate or satirise – he merely reports what he sees. Grange, Newholme, Meadowcroft, Heathcote, Langsmead, Runfold – they might have been coined just for him, rhymes or metaphors. And by the time you reach Camberley you are ready to be introduced to the inhabitants of his poems.

> Miss J. Hunter Dunn, Miss J. Hunter Dunn,
> Furnish'd and burnish'd by Aldershot sun,
> What strenuous singles we played after tea,
> We in the tournament – you against me!

> Love-thirty, love-forty, oh! weakness of joy,
> The speed of a swallow, the grace of a boy,
> With carefullest carelessness, gaily you won,
> I am weak from your loveliness, Joan Hunter Dunn.

In 1940 John Betjeman worked at the Ministry of Information, headquartered in the University of London Senate House. The deputy catering manageress had clear, slightly sunburned skin, brown eyes and brown curly hair, dark eyebrows – a strong girl in her early twenties, sturdily built, an in-charge sort of person, first aid and organisation, feeding between one and two thousand people. She had been to the University of London before the war, courses in domestic and social sciences. She was ten years younger than Betjeman when he met her – and even before they spoke he had convinced himself and his friends that she was a doctor's daughter from Aldershot. Which she was – a two-car, chauffeured family, sturdy Victorian residence. In school, Joan Hunter Dunn was head girl of her house, good at games.

> Miss Joan Hunter Dunn, Miss Joan Hunter Dunn,
> How mad I am, sad I am, glad that you won.
> The warm-handled racket is back in its press,
> But my shock-headed victor, she loves me no less.

> Her father's euonymus shines as we walk,
> And swing past the summer-house, buried in talk,
> And cool the verandah that welcomes us in
> To the six-o'clock news and a lime-juice and gin.

Everything about Joan Hunter Dunn appealed to John Betjeman. She was sweet and lively, strong and cool; she lived in the home counties, Farnborough in Hampshire between Aldershot and Camberley. Her background had the ingredients Betjeman fantasised – lacrosse in school, tennis at the large house of a friend, dances with the officers in the nearby Army towns.

> The Hillman is waiting, the light's in the hall,
> The pictures of Egypt are bright on the wall,
> My sweet, I am standing beside the oak stair
> And there on the landing's the light on your hair.

> By roads "not adopted", by woodlanded ways,
> She drove to the club in the late summer haze,
> Into nine-o'clock Camberley, heavy with bells
> And mushroomy, pine-woody, evergreen smells.

Contrary to the poem, John Betjeman and Joan Hunter Dunn did not fall in love. The tennis court came from The Mead, Wantage; it is still there, elevated and macadamed.

He never became a subaltern, but the Battle of Britain and the tales from northern France had filled the popular imagination with shy, fair-haired, young heroes, fighting their war in the skies or returning, stiff-upper-lipped and smoke-stained, from the front. Betjeman's song of love in a Surrey valley was divulged to Joan Hunter Dunn in the back of a taxi; he took her to lunch to advise her nervously that he had written a poem about her. She, in the dark days of war, was enthralled.

> Around us are Rovers and Austins afar,
> Above us, the intimate roof of the car,
> And here on my right is the girl of my choice,
> With the tilt of her nose and the chime of her voice,

> And the scent of her wrap, and the words never said,
> And the ominous, ominous dancing ahead.
> We sat in the car park till twenty to one
> And now I'm engaged to Miss Joan Hunter Dunn.

Today Joan Hunter Dunn lives not far away from Aldershot. The place of her girlhood, Farnborough, was more convenient for dancing in "nine-o'clock Camberley". The official handbook of Camberley Heath golf club has omitted to mention that momentous, summer evening of haze, pine-woody smells and love, but the club had provided all the facilities and still displays a pride in its reputation as "the spiritual home of Army golf . . . All round the rough and the nicely placed bunkers by the greens, are heather, bracken, and Surrey's omnipresent pine trees, and here and there birches to set off the general shades of green. The greens are not just the usual sand-country greens, hard, fast, and true. Long years of greenkeeping under the genius Robinson, and the comparable genius of his successor Tony Williams, have produced something a little bit more subtle. There is, on most holes, a nicely calculated springiness of surface so that the well hit iron shot will bite and hold most decisively. The club house stands upon a crest of the pine country, just off the main road from London which branches left at the Jolly Farmer, between Bagshot and Camberley. The Club drive stands at the 29th milestone from Hyde Park Corner."

And, most important for evenings of dance and romance, the official handbook concludes: "Neither Secretary, club house,

catering nor staff need any bush at all. The visitor can emphatically and rightly take them for granted."

The most recent poem which John Betjeman placed specifically in these calm avenues appeared in *A Nip in the Air*, 1974. A leaflet, obtainable from the Rushmoor Borough Council, at the town hall in Farnborough, gives full directions. "The Park Crematorium lies to the south of Aldershot, below the northern slopes of the Hog's Back, on the south-eastern boundary of the borough of Aldershot. It is approached by a driveway leading from Guildford Road, off Lower Farnham Road, part of the A324 Farnham to Woking Road. The crematorium is well sign-

posted from various parts of the borough." Triangular flower beds, rose bushes, tall isolated trees, stand warily round the low brick building, keeping their distance from the crematorium chimney.

> Between the swimming-pool and cricket-ground
> How straight the crematorium driveway lies!
> And little puffs of smoke without a sound
> Show what we loved dissolving in the skies,
> Dear hands and feet and laughter-lighted face
> And silk that hinted at the body's grace.

The official leaflet strikes a note somewhere between the respectful and the merrily factual. "What YOU should know about Cremation." Lists of advantages appeal to the conscientious: YOU should know "that cremation is recognised by Public Health Authorities as the most hygienic method of disposal of the dead. That the continued provision of new burial ground prevents the economic use of valuable land for housing, slum clearance and playing fields. That, since cremation is an indoor ceremony, the mourners are not exposed to the inclemencies of the weather." And death shall have no dominion – only bureaucracy.

> But no-one seems to know quite what to say
> (Friends are so altered by the passing years):
> "Well, anyhow, it's not so cold today" –
> And thus we try to dissipate our fears.
> *I am the Resurrection and the Life:*
> Strong, deep and painful, doubt inserts the knife.

The drive back to London along the A321 takes you to Farnborough, where Joan Hunter Dunn was a strongly adorable tennis girl, to Camberley, where the young subaltern had a view from his bedroom of moss-dappled path. Are there pictures of Egypt bright on the walls of the houses – and does the six-o'clock news still accompany the lime-juice and gin? Or has the puff of smoke from Aldershot crematorium become a cloud?

> Fling wide the curtains! – that's a Surrey sunset
> Low down the line sings the Addiscombe train,
> Leaded are the windows lozenging the crimson,
> Drained dark the pines in resin-scented rain.

CHAPTER
EIGHT
THE
SEASIDE

Whether we like to sit with Penguin books
In sheltered alcoves farther up the cliff,
Or to eat winkles on the Esplanade,
Or to play golf along the crowded course,
Or on a twopenny borough council chair
To doze away the strains of *Humoresque*,
Adapted for the cornet and the drums
By the conductor of the Silver Band . . .

Citizens of Betjeman country find the South Coast bracing. Boroughs of wrought-iron railings, municipal azaleas and scabious, sandals with socks, ketchup with meat tea, bandstands with oompah and cymbals, salad days and pierrots on the pier – the annual seaside resort is a ritual place.

Twenty years ago as he invented Motopolis to bewail Oxford, and Trepolport to warn Cornwall, John Betjeman devised Flinthaven, a mythical south-coast collage of Margate, Broadstairs, Hastings, Eastbourne.

Flinthaven was a fishing cove until George III took the seawater cure at Weymouth. Fashion and, eventually, the railway brought the people to the seaside: "thereafter Flinthaven spread in all directions. A new big hotel in red terra cotta, called The Imperial, was built on the cliff-top in 1890 . . . Alexandra Park, named after the wife of the Prince of Wales, was laid out on some unremunerative land at the back of the town near the gasworks. A shopping arcade of red brick with green copper domes on its corners was built near the station. A pier and an esplanade were constructed on the front. All this was done before 1914."

Flinthaven's "semi-detached, gabled, three-storey houses with bay windows for viewing the sea" were a day trip from London – but how much more comforting was August's habitual wish-you-were-here.

> Still the quartz
> Glitters along the tops of gardens walls.

It does, it does!

> Still the shops
> Remain unaltered on the Esplanade –
> The Circulating Library, the Stores,
> Jill's Pantry, Cynthia's Ditty Box (Antiques)

A Souvenir of Flinthaven.

> Still on the terrace of the big hotel
> Pale pink hydrangeas turn a rusty brown
> Where sea winds catch them, and yet do not die.

Like Aertex sleeveless shirts, like striped deckchairs, Flinthaven, from year to year, does not change.

Slam the door,
And pack the family in the Morris eight.
Lock up the garage. Put her in reverse,
Back out with care, now, forward, off – away!
The richer people living farther out
O'ertake us in their Rovers. We, in turn,
Pass poorer families hurrying on foot
Towards the station.

The A21 from London today is not a boastful road, no flash
and roar of motorway. Rather it is a civil servant of a road,
sometimes helpful, sometimes obstructive. Past oasthouses,
woods, farms, through dormitory towns and dormer villages the
A21 winds thoughtfully down to the South Coast. On its mar-
gins dwell the commuting generations of Betjeman people, in
red-tiled bungalows and neo-Georgian developments, Cedar
Gables, Forest Lawns, Oak Spinney. Campari-and-soda and
vodka-and-tonic please, and you can murder a pint of real ale
in the Royal Oak or the Hare and Hounds.

I am a young executive. No cuffs than mine are cleaner;
I have a Slimline brief-case and I use the firm's Cortina.
In every roadside hostelry from here to Burgess Hill
The *maîtres d'hôtel* all know me well and let me sign the bill.

Near Burgess Hill you can buy fresh eggs and Jersey cream
at Poplar Farm; in the villages, Pratt's Bottom, Hook Green,
Lamberhurst, antique shops sells fenders and firebaskets; small
churches and fingerposts suggest Normandy. Sliced escarp-
ments of beige clay, thin sudden retinues of poplar and conifer
and aspen – the land is farmed pecuniously, fat cattle, and neat
manors of hayricks.
   The names on the signs make a child-distracting litany – Eastbourne, Bexhill, Hastings, St. Leonards, Rye, how many more
miles to Flinthaven?

And, at that moment, Jennifer is sick
(Over-excitement must have brought it on,
The hurried breakfast and the early start)
And Michael's rather pale, and as for Anne . . .
"Please stop a moment, Hubert, anywhere."

Nose to the car window: eaved heights of houses, Victorian,
pebble-dashed or half-timbered, a municipal, discreet park, no
bicycles allowed, seats with commemorating plaques, young
tennis; diamond-patterned linoleum in the hallway, a hatstand

with a centre mirror – timeless Flinthaven, the holiday home of Betjeman country, is a stern landlady of ample, gowned bosom.

Still on the bedroom wall, the list of rules:
Don't waste the water. It is pumped by hand.
Don't throw old blades into the W.C.
Don't keep the bathroom long and don't be late
For meals and don't hang swim-suits out on sills
(A line has been provided at the back).
Don't empty children's sand-shoes in the hall.

(The Canadian humorist, Stephen Leacock, figured that the landlady is a geometric figure, a parallelogram, i.e. an angular oblong figure which cannot be described and which is equal to anything, and pie may be produced to infinity.)

A postcard from Flinthaven is a self-portrait of Hastings. The foreshore is three miles long, striped with hotels and boarding-houses and cafes, "Take a seat or Take away". Hastings pier juts out into the grey-green water, a half-hearted, ornate, forgotten bridge to France. Nine hundred feet long, a Palace-on-the-Sea, begun in December 1869, it took two and a half years to complete (turnstiles by W. T. Ellison & Co., Irlam-o-th'-Height, Manchester). When it opened, on the 5th of August, 1872, galantines of beef were served, and lobster, Leeds pudding and blancmange; champagne was seven shillings and sixpence a bottle, and sixty coastguards formed a guard of honour while the band of the Royal Marine Artillery played rousing music. It was Britain's first statutory Bank Holiday – it rained.

And poured – the pier was severely damaged by fire in 1917, the Pavilion took five years to rebuild. In 1939 it was bisected in case Hitler used it as a gangplank – in the footsteps of William the Conqueror – and it was subsequently bombed. Its repaired piecemeal appearance is sad now, with bingo and fishermen; rust stains the white paint. Kathy McKay, the Clairvoyante-Palmiste of Celtic Romany origin, offers a sober warning to fortune-seeking girls.

If some man you think you'll wed
Don't be hasty, use your head
At first his failings may not show
But day by day perhaps they'll grow
Before you wear his golden band
Let me analyse his hand.

Was it always two weeks in August? Betjeman beside the seaside is a fortnight of goosefleshed feast days.

The morning paddle, then the mystery tour
By motor-coach inland this afternoon.
For that old mother what a happy time!
At last past bearing children, she can sit
Reposeful on a crowded bit of beach.

But the enjoyment was more in the anticipation and the later recollection than in the experience. In the annually unexpected listlessness, family foibles embarrassingly became magnified into novelettes, in the whispering goldfish-bowl of the fortnight's accommodation.

Oh! then what a pleasure to see the ground floor
With tables for two laid as tables for four,
And bottles of sauce and Kia-Ora and squash
Awaiting their owners who'd gone up to wash –

Who had gone up to wash the ozone from their skins
The sand from their legs and the Rock from their chins,
To prepare for an evening of dancing and cards
And forget the sea-breeze on the dry promenades.

The holiday makers in Betjeman's Flinthaven did not
quite get away from it all. Class travelled too; Grand Hotel,
"Private hotel", and boarding-house all measured the
changing fortunes of the people who returned year after
year.

Whether we own a tandem or a Rolls,
Whether we Rudge it or we trudge it, still
A single topic occupies our minds.
'Tis hinted at or boldly blazoned in
Our accents, clothes and ways of eating fish,
And being introduced and taking leave,
"Farewell", "So Long", "Bunghosky", "Cheeribye" –
That topic all-absorbing, as it was
Is now and ever shall be, to us – CLASS.

No longer – in Flinthaven the stucco is peeling, the brick needs repointing, the wrought-iron railings are rusting. Prosperity is several coats of paint away. The kiss-me-quick hats have been replaced by violent, coloured combs of hair, above painted, ear-ringed faces. The fortune hunters of Kathy McKay, Clairvoyante-Palmiste are off, having their lightning portraits drawn on the hot streets of some Costa.

Romans, Anglo Saxons, Normans, trippers, punks and now pensioners, have all invaded Betjeman's Flinthaven. The windy walks along the chalk cliffs, the crunching across the shingle, the cold paddling on the wide beaches – generation after generation has braved the bathing machines, the beach chalets, the bingo. On the old side of the town the original fishermen's cottages can still be seen, some occupied by natives, some with primary colours on the front doors owned by trendy young couples, he in advertising, she in the media. In the shopping arcades expensive boutiques gleam. The castle has had some rooms restored, wenches in mobcaps serve mead at medieval banquets.

John Betjeman was impressed by Brighton – "the best-looking seaside town in Britain", engaged by Southend – "sky and cloud formation, sunset and storm and constantly changing light", in love with Bournemouth – "the blue veins of her body are the asphalt paths meandering down her chines, among firs and sandy cliffs, her life-blood is the young and old who frequent them, the young running gaily up in beach shoes, the old wheeled steadily down in invalid chairs."

The nannies have gone, the Michaels, Annes, Christabels, Jennifers, grown up; fewer games of rounders on the beach, but in Betjeman country the seaside is Flinthaven for ever, safe and windy and wet and embarrassing and timeless.

> And all the time, the waves, the waves, the waves
> Chase, intersect and flatten on the sand
> As they have done for centuries, as they will
> For centuries to come, when not a soul
> Is left to picnic on the blazing rocks,
> When England is not England, when mankind
> Has blown himself to pieces.

CHAPTER
NINE
BERKSHIRE
AND
OXFORDSHIRE

I like the way these old brick garden walls
Unevenly run down to Letcombe Brook.
I like the mist of green about the elms
In earliest leaf-time. More intensely green
The duck-weed undulates; a mud-grey trout
Hovers and darts away at my approach.

The old brick garden walls still stand at the Mead, in Wantage – the elms, victims to disease, have gone; but the house is much as he left it, Oxford now, Berkshire then, the rural idyll of Betjeman country.

Before Wantage, newly wed John and Penelope Betjeman lived in the village of Uffington. Forty years later the village held a festival to commemorate a native son, Thomas Hughes, author of *Tom Brown's Schooldays*, also the Liberal Member for Lambeth, then Frome. The president of the festival, by then a famous poet, but long since left the village, wrote a message for the programme: "With its octagonal Tower, cross shaped church of stone and pebble-dash, surrounding cottages with

thatched roofs and clunch walls, towering elms and little streams and willows and footpaths, Uffington is the pride of the Vale of the White Horse. The line of the Downs to the South, the gentle rise of farmland to the limestone ridge of Faringdon and the harmless intrusion of the beloved Great Western Railway which first brought it within reach of London, Uffington has remained mercifully real Berkshire as it was in the time of Thomas Hughes."

Not so much blink, as nod off, and you would miss it: with a delicious rural tact Uffington sends strangers on their way in a circular fashion. If you approach it from the Oxfordshire border, by road from Wantage, the village lies in the crook of its own arm, between the peace of the church and the heights of the white horse on the downs.

> The old Great Western Railway shakes
> The old Great Western Railway spins –
> The old Great Western Railway makes
> Me very sorry for my sins.

Rumbling away in the distance the train which brought him down from London, to Garrard's Farm, a long, low house opposite the Fox and Horses.

John Betjeman was a churchwarden in Uffington. St. Mary's Church was his beloved; in 1937 he paid for the cleaning of the Royal Arms, later, presided over the conversion of the oil lamps to electricity. The church, cruciform, stands on a small height, apart, behind trees, a tower of character, round from a distance, octagonal upon closer acquaintance. The historian

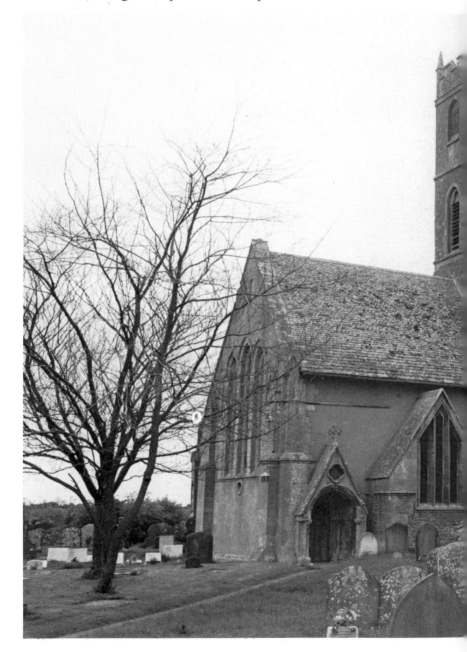

of Uffington, Mr. John E. Little, has recorded: "It is one of the finest examples of early English period, being all of that date except one window inserted in the 14th century and the upper part of the tower, which is modern. This replaced a spire, destroyed during a very severe gale in 1740 . . ."

Is a writer with a powerful sense of place drawn ineluctably

to a place with a sense of power? Uffington, for all its sleepy complexion, exudes a force which might be supernatural, is certainly the accumulation of historical mystery. The names associated with the village call forth bronzed mythological and violently possessive images. Wieland the Smith, who forged wings on his anvil, lent his mighty Norse aura to Wayland's Barrow – over the years the chalky ground here has, with great reluctance, yielded up Stone Age relics. And the white horse lopes surrealistically across the hillside, harsh and jagged, keeping its past to itself. Does it commemorate an ancient goddess – or King Alfred versus the Danes? And did St. George and the dragon not fight fiercely here too? And will the grass still not grow on the hillock where spilt the dragon's blood? Thomas Hughes, whose grandfather was vicar, is commemorated in St. Mary's Church, and in the churchyard lie several members of a ubiquitous family called Thatcher.

On the 1st of September, 1966, at 7.55 pm, the Week's Good Cause on the BBC was broadcast by John Betjeman; who else would begin, "Frankly we are bust in Uffington"? In its column, "Faringdon Focus", the *Wiltshire Gazette and Herald*, the 15th of September, 1966, reported, "The total in response to the radio appeal for Uffington Parish Church has reached £875. This is far above any figure anticipated by the vicar – or by John Betjeman who made the appeal." And the parish still credits the poet for the revival of the Mummers Plays.

> Tonight we feel the muffled peal
>   Hang on the village like a pall;
> It overwhelms the towering elms –
>   That death-reminding dying fall;
> The very sky no longer high
>   Comes down within the reach of all
> Imprisoned in a cage of sound
> Even the trivial seems profound.

Just one short poem called "Uffington" – no more; John Betjeman has not recollected the village poetically in any greater substance. In his broadcast alphabet of English churches "U" was for Uffington – otherwise his life here was unlabelled.

As an entity, though, the country village, such as Uffington, wrought its own importance in his work, despite his need for the protein of more formal architecture. Uffington was typical of the Wiltshire villages to which Betjeman the schoolboy had cycled on painting expeditions from Marlborough. The Englishness, the old words, the cottage history, the colours of the hinterland, became a rustic grist, a living Domesday Book. Progress, though tasteless and reprehensible, was somehow to be expected in the cities, but abhorrent in the intimate life of the countryside. "Pylons are higher and stride further," he shouted. "Grand new motorways bisect the little hills. Power stations browse in the meadows and wild places are sown with atomic energy plants. We are creating a landscape of power with its own, and no doubt fine, aesthetic interest. But it is on a superhuman scale and unrelated to what we think of as home. As the familiar outlines, high street, villages, farm buildings, trees and fields disappear, we realise we are losing part of ourselves."

His verses yelled, too. "The Dear Old Village" did not specify Uffington, nor Berkshire, nor Oxfordshire, nor any county: its existence was imaginary. Flinthaven again, Trepolport, Motopolis with thatched roofs and weekend wellies.

> Farmers have wired the public rights-of-way
> Should any wish to walk to church to pray.
> Along the village street the sunset strikes
> On young men tuning up their motor-bikes,
> And country girls with lips and nails vermilion
> Wait, nylon-legged, to straddle on the pillion.
> Off to the roadhouse and the Tudor Bar
> And then the Sunday-opened cinema.
> While to the church's iron-studded door
> Go two old ladies and a child of four.

Uffington still retains some of the older charms, even if the white horse on the inevitable pub sign bears no anatomical relation to the animal splayed across the hillside. The farms run their yards right up to the village street and tractors negotiate Workhouse Corner with patience – and wary anticipation, of the London-owned BMW. The local welcome is warm, hollows of comfort in the accent: Uffington seems safe from Betjemanesque dear-old-village grotesques:

> See that square house, late Georgian and smart,
> Two fields away it proudly stands apart,
> Dutch barn and concrete cow-sheds have replaced
> The old thatched roof which once the yard disgraced.
> Here wallows Farmer WHISTLE in his riches,
> His ample stomach heaved above his breeches.
> You'd never think that in such honest beef
> Lurk'd an adulterous braggart, liar and thief.

The journey by car – join the B4507 – from Uffington to Wantage is a leafy matter of mere miles. On foot it rewards more richly – through fields lower than the southern distant Ridge-way, past yew trees at farmers' gates, by stableyards and cot-tages, on footpaths by the early summer headlands of yellow oil-seed fields. To the right hides the tiny village of Kingston Lisle. In the grassed-over clay by a fence a rusted spar from a redundant implement; the houses settle into the folds and cor-ners of the acres untroubled for centuries, such a tailored land – untouched by war or dispute, a country that has not lately known invasion. The cattle mix, dairy and meat; farms, unde-monstratively rich, racing stables, sleek, shod and polished.

Wantage lies among trees, a local agricultural headquarters, fully serviced – except for tea on Sunday afternoons. In the Mar-ket Square, Arbery & Son, after their fashion, advertise, window by window, corsets, millinery, costumes, mantles; the statue of King Alfred gazes down at the parked cars – he was born here, defeated the Danes by linguistics, gave them the English lan-guage in return for peace. At the end of Church Street SS. Peter and Paul, thirteenth-century, cruciform, dim: aside from a chris-tening an elderly churchwarden whispers directions to the address of John Betjeman – "O – the former parishioner."

> Now with the bells through the apple bloom
> Sunday-ly sounding
> And the prayers of the nuns in their chapel gloom
> Us all surrounding,
> Where the brook flows
> Brick walls of rose
> Send on the motionless meadow the bell notes rebounding.

The Mead still conceals itself, even acting on the crow-flying instructions from the churchyard. Inconspicuous gate, shared with other houses, and the lane descends between hedges and high grasses, to outbuildings which shield the dwelling. Ahead, trees mask distant neighbours, the field drops sharply to water, and rounding the corner the house, neat but confusing, shows no change from its Betjeman years.

To the front, suggesting railway architecture, a brick Victor-ian villa, pointed porch, tall, mildly arched double windows, one on either side of the door at both ground-floor and upper-storey level – with a fifth single window surmounting the point of the porch. Round another corner, the original building, a farm house with "1762" scratched by the door, sits low and sheltered between the Victorian addition and the outbuildings. Lawns, terraced now, and adventurously water-gardened, reach away towards the trees; this pocket territory is lush and green and silent.

Wall flowers are bright in their beds
And their scent all pervading,
Withered are primroses heads
And the hyacinth fading
But flowers by the score
Multitudes more
Weed flowers and seed flowers and mead flowers our paths
are invading.

The Betjemans kept horses here too, and played tennis: the tennis court in the high corner suggests inspiration for more than one blonde Amazon:

Oh! would I were her racket press'd
With hard excitement to her breast
And swished into the sunlit air
Arm-high above her tousled hair,
And banged against the bounding ball
"Oh! Plung!" my tauten'd strings would call,
"Oh! Plung! my darling, break my strings
For you I will do brilliant things."

When ladies' magazines visited the Betjemans to investigate "living in the country" they found a house "bursting with character and with the personalities of its owners.

"There has been no conscious effort to furnish it in any particular period but a kaleidoscope of antiques, and modern aids to comfortable living combine in complete harmony." Chintz and William Morris carried the day, books came in a close second, "the harlequin patterns made by their bright backs complemented by the muted colours of the furnishings". Deep royal blue on the walls, red carpet on the floor, a marble bust of Queen Louise of Prussia in a staircase alcove, cyclamen walls and a rust-coloured floor in the family bathroom – the lady from the ladies' magazine recognised Betjeman country when she saw it.

Where are the words to express
Such a reckless bestowing?
The voices of birds utter less
Than the thanks we are owing,
Bell notes alone
Ring praise of their own
As clear as the weed-waving brook and as evenly flowing.

Curiously the time spent in Wantage and Uffington has left no huge impression upon John Betjeman's poetry; a few poems, occasional passing mention, nothing cerebral – thin fruit for twenty years of residence. The house was busy with visitors: Evelyn Waugh brought port and pique, the vicar drank sherry, the great Wally Hammond shaped strokes on the lawn, and the poet dispensed school boaters to summer guests, reserving a Harrow model for himself. He maintained rooms in London for much of the time – letters to parish officials in Uffington bear the Smithfield address "Cloth Fair".

Betjeman's professional life was carved out while he lived in this countryside. In 1934 he became a film critic on the *Evening Standard* in London: his five most important collections of verse were published while he was still domiciled here, *Continual Dew*, 1937, *Old Lights for New Chancels*, 1940, *New Bats in Old Belfries*, 1945, *Selected Poems*, 1948, *A Few Late Chrysanthemums*, 1954. *Summoned by Bells* was drafted during this period. The Shell Guides, the Murray's Architectural Guides, the innumerable broadcasts – all the reputations he sought to establish budded during his country living. Uffington, Wantage, Faringdon, the lanes and chalk ridges, were rural retreats.

As an observer he made the most of it, although all the times were not happy. While he lived near Wantage, Evelyn Waugh mounted a barrage of letters in an effort to make John Betjeman convert to Roman Catholicism. The attack was fierce: hell was threatened, reason was questioned. Penelope Betjeman eventually had to write to Waugh asking him to desist; John was having nightmares. She, though, became a Catholic in 1948, was received at St. Aloysius, Oxford, to Waugh's delight, to John's chagrin. Of the two poems directly related to Wantage, one, "On Leaving Wantage, 1972", reflects his bewilderment.

> Suddenly on the unsuspecting air
> The bells clash out. It seems a miracle
> That leaf and flower should never even stir
> In such great waves of medieval sound:
> They ripple over roofs to fields and farms
> So that "the fellowship of Christ's religion"
> Is roused to breakfast, church or sleep again.
>
> From this wide vale, where all our married lives
> We two have lived, we now are whirled away
> Momently clinging to the things we knew –
> Friends, footpaths, hedges, house and animals –
> Till, borne along like twigs and bits of straw,
> We sink below the sliding stream of time.

CHAPTER
TEN
BATH
AND
BRISTOL

Now houses are "units" and people are digits,
And Bath has been planned into quarters for midgets.
Official designs are aggressively neuter,
The Puritan work of an eyeless computer.

In *First and Last Loves*, the architectural essays published in 1952, John Betjeman wrote, "We accept the collapse of the fabrics of our old churches, the thieving of lead and objects from them, the commandeering and butchery of our scenery by the services, the despoiling of landscaped parks and the abandonment to a fate worse than the workhouse of our country houses, because we are convinced we must save money." In the poem, "Inexpensive Progress", the knife went in much deeper:

> Encase your legs in nylons,
> Bestride your hills with pylons
> O age without a soul;

All his life, since those childhood years in which he believed that, yes, this was, as the guide said, the bed in which Queen Elizabeth I slept, Betjeman's alternative religion has been architecture. At the age of twelve, when other boys were playing cricket or reading "shockers", he was discovering and exploring ignored or forgotten jewels of church architecture. Different teachers, Gerald Haynes in Oxford, Christopher Hughes the art master in Marlborough, had drawn his eye to such finer things. At university, he bought Professor Richardson's *Monumental Classic Architecture in Great Britain and Ireland*. "There were, of course, the officially approved books on officially approved architecture, that is to say Jacobean and early English Renaissance and the work of Lutyens and the gardens for early Lutyens houses laid out by Miss Jekyll. These, however, were less interesting to me than what could then be bought for five or ten shillings at the many suburban and provincial secondhand bookshops which then abounded. Here I found late eighteenth-century and early nineteenth-century books of designs for lodges, villas and country mansions, illustrated with sepia and sometimes with coloured aquatints."

Morality, of all things, inspired John Betjeman's love of buildings. Old values, stability, graciousness – in architecture these qualities were offered their most public manifestation, tangible, visible citadels of what was good and safe and fine. "For architecture means not a house, or a single building or a church," he lectured, "but our surroundings, not a town or a street, but our whole over-populated island. It is concerned with where we eat, work, sleep, play, congregate, escape." Other poets chose mythology for their themes and were called "great": Betjeman chose everyday, living values and valuations and was christened "popular". For Ulysses, Apollo, Adonis read Lutyens, Gilbert Scott and – revised but lately – Norman Shaw.

Of all the gay Places the World can afford,
By Gentle and Simple for Pastime ador'd,
Fine Balls, and fine Concerts, fine Buildings, and Springs,
Fine Walks, and fine Views, and a Thousand fine Things
(Not to mention the sweet Situation and Air),
What Place, my dear Mother, with *Bath* can compare?

Surprisingly enough, not John Betjeman: Christopher Anstey in 1766 wrote, *The New Bath Guide*, a collection of letters in verse written home, as it were, to describe the antics of the Blunderhead family on a visit to take the waters.

I'm sure I have travell'd our Country all o'er
And ne'er was so civilly treated before;
You never can go, my dear Mother, where you
So much have to see, and so little to do.

In *A Nip in the Air*, published in 1974, Betjeman brought Anstey up to date with "The Newest Bath Guide".

It is two hundred years since he got in his stride
And cantered away with *The New Bath Guide*.
His spondees and dactyls had quite a success,
And sev'ral editions were called from the press.
That guidebook consisted of letters in rhyme
On the follies and fashions of Bath at the time:
I notice a quiver come over my pen
As I think of the follies and fashions since then . . .

Not all cities deserve the pronoun "she". Bath does. Sired by the Romans, wedded by the Georgians, she sits on her skirts by the Avon, creamed and smoothed down in a buff stone. The Roman spring brought Aquae Sulis from the Mendip Hills, waters from a Celtic goddess; Queen Anne found them beneficial, and Bath, an inconspicuous and ailing wool town, cashed in. And dressed up – John Wood the Younger began the magnificent ellipse of Royal Crescent in 1767, thirty houses, a hundred and fourteen Ionic columns, two hundred yards and eight years. Five of the houses remain in private hands – investments of grandeur.

Number 1, Royal Crescent has been rescued from time, is again a Georgian household. High, light-filled rooms, doors and staircases wide to admit hooped skirts and sedans, thin-stalked Hepplewhite furniture delicate as flowers, table furnishings meticulously strewn. A rummer on the mantel, a decanter on the library table; candlestick, small books in the peaceful blue bedroom, and for the toilette, a small bowl; miniatures on the wall, a deep deep bed. Notwithstanding the tourists, the stillness here may be inhaled with benefit.

> The Towns of *Devizes*, of *Bradford* and *Frome*,
> May boast that they better can manage the Loom;
> I believe that they may; but the World to refine,
> In Manners, in Dress, in Politeness to shine,
> *O Bath*! let the Art, let the Glory be thine.

Six years after Christopher Anstey wrote to his mother there was an incident at Number 11, Royal Crescent, when the daughter of the house, Elizabeth, "eloped with Richard Brinsley Sheridan on the evening of the 18th of March, 1772". At Number 14, a stone frog sits guard; at Number 16, now The Royal Crescent Hotel, the bell, mystifyingly superfluously, requests "Please do not ring unless an answer is required". At

Number 17, there is a small commemoration of Sir Isaac Pitman, who devised a form of shorthand. Obviously it survives – the plaque merely offers that he was born in 1813 and died in 1887. And at Number 22 a supplication: "Don't let your dog put a dirty mark on Britain."

Proud City of Bath with your crescents and squares,
Your hoary old Abbey and playbills and chairs,
Your plentiful chapels where preachers would preach
(And a different doctrine expounded in each),
Your gallant assemblies where squires took their daughters,
Your medicinal springs where their wives took the waters,
The terraces trim and the comely young wenches,
The cobbled back streets with their privies and stenches –
   How varied and human did Bath then appear
   As the roar of the Avon rolled up from the weir.

Under Pulteney Bridge the Avon flows changeably: the city arcades sell chocolate, jeans, kitchenware. Georgian Duke Street is paved and paced and self-conscious – peeped into from across the city by bungalows gawking at such style.

   In those days, no doubt, there was not so much taste:
   But now there's so much it has all run to waste
   In working out methods of cutting down cost –
   So that mouldings, proportion and texture are lost
   In a uniform nothingness.

Time after time Betjeman has attacked the architects, the high priests, the singers and their songs. "There are nearly 20,000 architects on the register of the Royal Institute," he wrote in 1960. "They cannot all be artists, although architecture is an art. Some think of themselves as planners. They are concerned how to fit a given number of people into a given space, for a given sum of money. Some have lapsed into the role of public relations officer and are employed to charm committees, overcome obstructions from government departments and local authorities or to take potential clients out to lunch . . . Still more will run up for you whatever you want. These employ men to produce flash perspectives to impress customers."

The local authoritarians came in for fiercer hostility. Years of sitting on conservation committees, leading campaigns to preserve old buildings (he never forgave the Macmillan government for pulling down the Euston Arch in London, still steams at the memory) distilled Betjeman's contempt, hatred, even, for planners whose spirit did not extend to heritage or beauty.

   The first-class brains of a senior civil servant
      Shiver and shatter and fall
   As the steering column of his comfortable Humber
      Batters in the bony wall.
   All those delicate little re-adjustments

"On the one hand, if we proceed
With the *ad hoc* policy hitherto adapted
To individual need . . .
On the other hand, too rigid an arrangement
Might, of itself, perforce . . ."

Betjeman's rage stirred a consciousness. His campaigns
embraced towns, villages, churches, mansions, skylines, and
where the planners and builders beat him to it he was rueful.
And pessimistic: "It remains to be seen what more our own inde-
cisive age of internal combustion and nuclear physics will do
to Bath. The slabs of new flats off the London Road, the spreading suburbs, the new technical college are signs of the times.

No one can look at Royal Crescent and Lansdown Crescent
and the Pump Room without realising we once were civilised."
Betjeman's Bath exudes an anxious calm. The slow stupid march
of development, dull, heavy-footed, but dogged and dangerous,
bodes unease: will the pygmies gather round the pillars and,
in time, pull them down? If a prophet is denied honour will a
poet be heard?

Goodbye to old Bath! We who loved you are sorry
They're carting you off by developer's lorry.

Travel west ten miles – to Bristol. "Bristol has escaped the worst phases of nineteenth and twentieth-century industrialism," wrote Betjeman in 1961. "Though it was cruelly bombed in the last war, and the little churches and narrow lanes with their tall over-hanging houses in the centre of the city largely destroyed, Bristol is still for me the most beautiful, interesting and distinguished city in England."

A mazed city still, with fewer signposts than Alaska, a city of wide streets, quiet squares, docks with wistful names, Merchants Landing, Narrow Quay, from where traders, slavers, sailors of fortune put forth, jacktarring Bristol for ever with the romance of venture. Bristol captivated Betjeman. "I recall a ghost story about someone putting up for the night in a seventeenth-century Bristol house down by the waterside, and waking at two in the morning to hear the rumbling of barrels and loud Elizabethan oaths, and looking out to see a ship being manned and loaded to fight the Spanish Armada."

The docksides are lined now with restaurants and arts centres, with restored pubs and riverside houses, with capstans, cobblestones and old memories: only the ships are missing. The church of St. Mary Redcliffe was described by Queen Elizabeth I as

"the fairest, goodliest and most famous parish church in England". But this is a whole city of fair and goodly churches – All Saints, Corn Street; Christ Church, Broad Street; St. Mark, College Green; little Saint John the Baptist, Tower Lane; tall St. Paul, Portland Square – Betjeman, the guide to English churches, dances about Bristol.

Then all Somerset was round me and I saw the clippers ride,
High above the moonlit houses, triple-masted on the tide,
By the tall embattled church-towers of the Bristol waterside.

And an undersong to branches dripping into pools and wells
Out of multitudes of elm trees over leagues of hills and dells,
Was the mathematic pattern of a plain course on the bells.

Bristol is firmer and brisker than Bath, and it shows. "The differences between the eighteenth-century houses of Bristol and those of Bath are two," was Betjeman's moral judgment. "Bristol houses are often of brick with stone dressings, whereas Bath houses are all of stone with more impressive fronts; the Bath houses were mostly built as lodgings for the season, while the Bristol merchants' houses were built as permanent residences and money was lavished on their interiors."

When they had stopped living over the shop, that is. In 1884 *Arrowsmith's Directory* recorded that "On leaving the busy wharves of Bristol, the prospect of the Avon opens up like a romantic vision. The wrinkled, creviced and moss-grown precipices appearing, and symmetrical rows of hansome [sic] houses are piled storey after storey like the Hanging Gardens of Babylon." Clifton is a rich and elegant precinct, carved and corniced with tree-shaded lofty crescents and secluded squares. Royal York Crescent looks out to the hills, a general standing to attention: the wrought-iron balconies and capricious tubs of flowers uphold the Crescent's reputation as the longest in Europe. "The bankruptcy of the promoter in 1793," declaims a plaque, "brought work to a standstill, and in 1801 the government bought the ground and the unfinished portion of the Crescent, intending to build barracks. Local opposition frustrated this plan and the Crescent was completed in 1820 as originally envisaged."

Around the corner, on the way to Brunel's bridge, parkland opens out. A crazy monument, a haphazard, barren sarcophagus commemorates: "Sacred to the memory of those departing warriors of the seventy-ninth regiment by whose Valour, Discipline and Perseverance the French land forces in Asia were first withstood and repulsed. The Commerces of Great Britain preserved. Her settlements rescued from impending Destruction. The memorable Defence of MADRAS. The Decisive Battle of WANDEWASH. Twelve strong and important fortresses. Three superb capitals . . ." and concludes, "Their generous Treatment of a vanquished Enemy exhibits an illustrious example of true Fortitude and Moderation worthy of being transmitted to latest posterity that future generations may know HUMANITY is the Characteristic of BRITISH CONQUERORS."

By the park, on the left, the Clifton Down United Reform Church, then Gloucester Row and its jutting porches; over to the right, through the trees, on the slopes before the Avon Gorge, resolute, respectable houses keep their distance from the edge of the grass, dowagers by a shore. This is Cabot country: from Bristol and environs did John Cabot sail to discover Newfoundland and America – a year before Columbus landed, say the Chauvins of Bristol – and thence to intercede evermore between the Lowells and God. Paul Berg is the vicar of Christ Church "to whom wedding, baptism and banns applications should be made". (Again, not a word about funerals.) By the Chamber of Commerce – surely Bristol's temple? – across Cobblestone Mews, through opulent Worcester Terrace, Clifton's sheen gleams. "Bristol's biggest surprise is Clifton," Betjeman

confirmed, "a sort of Bath consisting of Regency crescents and terraces overlooking the Avon Gorge to the blue hills of Somerset. The finest of them in size is Royal York Crescent – the largest crescent in England – and there are many handsome late-Georgian terraces . . . Steep hills lead to steps: steps lead to terraces: and everywhere there are glimpses of gardens, delicate verandahs, lawns and trees. No English city has so large and leafy a suburb as Clifton. As the merchants climbed up the hill out of trade into the professions they moved to Clifton and from their Georgian houses went out to found the Empire . . ."

Pembroke Road is chock-full of cathedrals. The concrete-clad rectangular fingers of SS. Peter and Paul draw prayers down from the sky: inside, the baleful Stations of the Cross wrench every muscle on the climb to Calvary. Confessionals advertise the Sacrament of Reconciliation – "Anonymous Confession" or "Face to Face". Across Pembroke Road, by Alma Vale, a holy phoenix has risen: the old tower and the narthex of All Saints', Clifton, held their breath through the bombings of World War Two.

> "This is the window to my lady wife.
> You cannot see it now, but in the day
> The greens and golds are truly wonderful."
>
> "How very sad. I do not mean about
> The window, but I mean about the death
> Of Mrs. Battlecock. When did she die?"
>
> "Two years ago when we had just moved in
> To Pembroke Road."

All Saints', Clifton, is a decent and elegant church. Within the reconstituted body John Piper's stained-glass filaments embroider the walls. The high altar spans time and religion – the polished Portland stone is limned with fossil shells from a quarry in Dorset. All along the corridors, reflected in the glass windows of the atrium, the Kodachrome likenesses of the parishioners slowly fill the notice-boards, instamatic introductions by the shrine of Our Lady of Walsingham. Footsteps click in passageway, friendly swish of a black cassock.

> "We had
> A stained glass window on the stairs at home,
> In Pembroke Road. But not so good as this.
> This window is the glory of the church
> At least I think so – and the unstained oak
> Looks very chaste beneath it."

John Betjeman was only twenty-seven when he published *Ghastly Good Taste or a depressing story of the Rise and Fall of English Architecture* – a brave, impertinent book, which he revised in 1970. Baroque, awkward, outspoken and concerned, Betjeman's voice percussed through the prose. From genuine Tudor, through Jacobethan, Queen Anne, and Gothick, through Middle Class, Middle Class Self Conscious, Big Business and Chaos, Status Symbol and Science, Religion and the Space Age, he led his readers to a moral conclusion. "Architecture can only be made alive again by a new order and another Christendom." In Bristol he found such Christendom only by searching. "No one would know from the outside how remarkable was the inside of the Cathedral." In Bath, more admired than loved, he took the city's Georgian Jane Austen-ish presence as a gift, used the city's name – "In a Bath Teashop" – as an overhang.

> "Let us not speak, for the love we bear one another –
>   Let us hold hands and look."
> She, such a very ordinary little woman;
>   He, such a thumping crook;
> But both, for a moment, little lower than the angels
>   In the teashop's ingle-nook.

PART THREE

CHAPTER
ELEVEN
CHURCHES

Light six white tapers with the Flame of Art,
Send incense wreathing to the lily flowers,
And, with your cool hands white,
Swing the warm censer round my bruised heart,
Drop, dove-grey eyes, your penitential showers
On this pale acolyte.

Churches in all their variety – of architecture and worship – have long been John Betjeman's passion. They bulk as large in his mind, his heart, his spirit and his poems as the combined elements of the girls he loves and loved, the planning officials he tackled, the buildings he fought to save, the railways he explored, the suburbs he chronicled. From childhood he has cherished churches, enquired into them, sought them out.

He was born and baptised into a staunch Church of England family. At Marlborough and Oxford he drifted, was eventually drawn back, more aesthetically than theologically or devotionally. "I do see," he observed, years ago, "that behind all the ritual and everything like that, the one fundamental thing is that Christ was God. And it's very hard to believe – it's a very hard thing to swallow. But if you can believe it, it gives some point to everything and really I don't think life would be worth living if it weren't true." His commitment flowed over into his prose. In the outstandingly comprehensive *Collins Guide to Parish Churches of England and Wales*, which he first edited in 1958, his Introduction managed to be both informative and timeless.

"The Parish Churches of England are even more varied than the landscape. The tall town church, smelling of furniture polish and hot-water pipes, a shadow of the mediaeval marvel it once was, so assiduously have Victorian and even later restorers renewed everything old; the little weather-beaten hamlet church standing in a farmyard down a narrow lane, bat-droppings over the pews and one service a month; the church of a once prosperous village, a relic of the 15th-century wool trade, whose soaring splendour of stone and glass subsequent generations have had neither the energy nor the money to destroy; the suburban church with Northamptonshire-style steeple rising unexpectedly above slate roofs of London and calling with mid-Victorian bells to the ghosts of merchant carriage folk for whom it was built; the tin chapel-of-ease on the edge of the industrial estate; the High, the Low, the Central churches, the alive and the dead ones, the churches that are easy to pray in and those that are not, the churches whose architecture brings you to your knees, the churches whose decorations affront the sight – all these come within the wide embrace of our Anglican Church, whose arms extend beyond the seas to many fabrics more."

And there they stand, all across Betjeman country, like lighthouses, old decrepit friends or imposing cousins, each one with – in Betjeman's terms – its unique value, or warm welcome, or social, spiritual and historical significance.

With oh such peculiar branching and over-reaching of wire
   Trolley-bus standards pick their threads from the London sky
Diminishing up the perspective, Highbury-bound retire
   Threads and buses and standards with plane trees volleying by
And, more peculiar still, that ever-increasing spire
   Bulges over the housetops, polychromatic and high.

St. Saviour's, Aberdeen Park, Highbury, was the London church in which, for small John Betjeman, worship became synonymous with roots and social class.

This red-brick, loosely-enclaved neighbourhood looped off Highbury Grove pleads to be a private road, has not quite got the voice for it. Trees flourish in the necessary protective profusion, ramps jolt the speed and the noise out of disrespectful traffic. Mixed architecture, nineteenth-and-early-twentieth-century-North-London-satisfied, wide roads making houses standoffish, an absence of community-making shops, give Aberdeen Park an air somewhere between keeping itself to itself and over-ambitious or mistaken town planning.

Stop the trolley-bus, stop! And here, where the roads unite
   Of weariest worn-out London – cigarettes, no beer,
No repairs undertaken, nothing in stock – alight;
   For over the waste of willow-herb, look at her sailing clear,
A great Victorian church, tall unbroken and bright
   In a sun that's setting in Willesden and saturating us here.

These were the streets my parents knew when they loved and
                               won –
   The brougham that crunched the gravel, the laurel-girt paths
                           that wind,
Geranium-beds for the lawn. Venetian blinds for the sun,
   A separate tradesman's entrance, straw in the mews behind,
Just in the four-mile radius where hackney carriages run,
   Solid Italianate houses for the solid commercial mind.

The family's North London connections, professionally rooted in the furniture factory at Islington, had chosen the merchant style of living, the crests and plaques of Victorian, hard-working, God-fearing successful enterprise. Ernest and Bessie Betjemann may have gone to live in Highgate but their tribal headquarters remained in Highbury.

      Slow walks we took
   On sunny afternoons to great-great-aunts
   In tall Italianate houses: Aberdeen Park,

Hillmarton Road and upper Pooter-land,
Short gravel drives to steepish flights of steps
And stained-glass windows in a purple hall,
A drawing-room with stands of potted plants,
Lace curtains screening other plants beyond.

St. Saviour's appearance in the *Guide to Parish Churches* is brief: "White's red brick cruciform church of 1859 has a low octagonal lantern tower. The interior, red brick with low aisles and a painted chancel, is beautifully proportioned." Even such succinctness is now redundant. The incumbent of St. Saviour's, Mr. Brandreth, retired on the 23rd of May, 1982. Congregations had been dwindling, twenty, thirty worshippers – and this had been the case long before he went there; neither did many of those who prayed come from the immediate vicinity, rather they had kept on returning from the parishes to which they had moved. When Mr. Brandreth left, the brick cruciform church was closed, locked, fenced and boarded – a disconsolate mirror of the changed fortunes in such Victorian suburbs;

. . . where carriages used to throng
And my mother stepped out in flounces and my father
                              stepped out in spats
To shadowy stained-glass matins or gas-lit evensong
And back in a country quiet with doffing of chimney hats.

The gap in the planked fence suggests unofficial entry; debris, plastic bottles, a useless roofrack, a shoe, an old shirt, the spoor of vandalism. The windows are boarded up, the leaded lights of stained glass either stolen, or removed for protection; a loose and dishevelled wire bulb-holder hangs askew over the closed porch where a rain-stained local council notice goes unheeded and unread. Sycamore shoots sprout disrespectfully, a huge horse chestnut spreads its arms warmly towards the sloping roof. Soon this building must succumb to ecclesiastical decision or secular violation.

Great red church of my parents, cruciform crossing they
                              knew –
Over these same encaustics they and their parents trod
Bound through a red-brick transept for a once familiar pew
Where the organ set them singing and the sermon let them
                              nod
And up this coloured brickwork the same long shadows grew
As these in the stencilled chancel where I kneel in the
                              presence of God.

Since his early voyages of schoolboy discovery, by bicycle in Cornwall, by train around London, Betjeman has been on a mission – to explore and then divulge and share, with excitement and enthusiasm, his joy at the dimensions, architectural, spiritual, sociological and historical, of parish churches.

On the BBC West of England programme, on Wednesday, August the 31st, 1938, he told his listeners "How to Look at a Church". The text, vintage Betjeman, brought out all his loves and his prejudices. "There's something much kinder about a house which has been lived in for generations than a brand new one," he began, and developed the theme in relation to churches. "Old glass still diffuses the daylight on the latest hats as softly as it did on the wigs of the eighteenth century . . . Elizabethan silver is still used for the sacrament. And from the tower a bell cast soon after the Wars of the Roses lends its note to the peal that ripples over the meadows and threads its way under the drone of aeroplanes. The magniloquent epitaph and well-carved bust of some dead squire looks down in breathing marble from the walls, and the churchyard is a criss-cross of slanting old stones. Here lies the England we are all beginning to wish we knew, as the roar of the machine gets louder and the suburbs creep from London to Land's End."

The instructions with which he then proceeded included the exhortation to, "Forget that old bore who lectured you at school on Norman fonts, forget those long hours trying to distinguish between Early English and Decorated. I'll give you a rough and ready rule for all this."

And he did – down through the processions of the styles: Saxon, "not enough around for you to bother about", Norman, "round-headed arches and round stubby columns and thick walls", Gothic, "cannot be divided accurately into styles".

He filled the broadcast with absorbing information and guidance; all the important tombstones stand in that part of the churchyard to the south of the church in fear of the legend that the devil dwelt in the northern section, where, thus, only disgraced people were buried; or the rules by which a church might be gauged: "If there's a slight smell of incense and the *English Hymnal* is used and the church is open and easy to get into; if the altar has many candles on it and a curved and painted wood at the back called a reredos, and a glowing frontal, then the Church is 'High'. If there are only two candles and a brass cross on the altar and a couple of vases of flowers and a noncommittal frontal, then the church is 'Broad' or what is termed 'Ordinary'. If there is a bare table at the east end with an alms dish on it and a chair at the north side and a little reading stand on the table, then the church is 'Low'. Low churches are often

locked." Or were – Betjeman's mission has not reached the ears of those who vandalise open churches.

The church was locked, so I went to the incumbent –
the incumbent enjoying a supine incumbency –
a tennis court, a summerhouse, deckchairs by the walnut tree
and only the hum of the bees in the rockery.
"May I have the keys of the church, your incumbency?"

Visit five of the churches John Betjeman has written about – visit fifty. Find his quiet country parish churches, small places, cared for in a domestic fashion by the rector, his wife, his children, his cat. For such buildings John Betjeman has long been an unofficial Poet Laureate. When restoration was required in the Church of St. Katherine, Chiselhampton, Oxfordshire ("on the edge of a small park stands this little white church built 1763, complete with bell-cote and vane. Inside clear glass round-headed windows, box pews, carved wooden altar-piece, tablets and candles make an unspoiled interior"), he wrote a poem to appeal for funds.

And must that plaintive bell in vain
Plead loud along the dripping lane?
And must the building fall?
Not while we love the Church and live
And of our charity will give
Our much, our more, our all.

The continuity must be preserved: every detail of the village church is therefore worth recording. "Flapping with electoral rolls, notices of local acts, missionary appeals and church services . . ." he described the archetypal village-church porch in his *Parish Churches* Introduction: "Though the powers of the parish vestry have been taken over by parish councils and local government, church doors or the porches which shelter them are often plastered with public announcements. Regularly will the village policeman nail to the church door some notice about Foot-and-Mouth Disease when the British Legion Notice Board has been denied him or the Post Office is shut." How quickly he weaves the threads of history into a tapestry. "Most church porches in England are built on the south side, first as a protection for the door from prevailing south-west gales. Then they were used as places for baptism, bargains were made there, oaths sworn, and burial and marriage services conducted. Above some of them, from the 14th century onwards, a room was built, usually for keeping parish chests and records. In these places

many a village school was started. At first they may have been inhabited by a watchman, who could look down into the church from an internal window . . ."

Follow his directions and history reveals itself. A tiny, somewhat dishevelled church in Norfolk, near Ditchingham, holds the tomb of Rider Haggard under the carpet in the main aisle: the window is stained with medallions of glass depicting the houses he lived in (including an African farm), but alas, no portrait of his daughter upon whom L. P. Hartley based the girl in love for his novel, *The Go-Between.* In Minster Lovell, near Burford in Oxfordshire (described in the *Guide* as "Lovely setting near ruins of priory on banks of Windrush. Perpendicular; vaulted under central tower. Monuments and glass"), Lambert Simnel lurked in terror and the green was donated to the village by a Mrs. La Terriere. Coincidence? Could she possibly be the famous Irish huntswoman, Mrs. La Terriere, whose father Colonel Grubb is buried standing up in the Knockmealdown Mountains of County Waterford? And heaven only knows what happened to Betjeman's narrator in "A Lincolnshire Tale".

> Though myself the Archdeacon for many a year,
> I had not summoned courage for visiting here;
> Our incumbents were mostly eccentric or sad
> But – *the Speckleby Rector was said to be mad.*

What is it that he has been seeking? All those journeys down the rutted country lanes, through the long grasses of the churchyards, knocking on the doors of hollow-ringing rectories asking for the key – was it merely architectural and historical curiosity which drove him? Critics have discussed his sense of insecurity, argue that he has needed the protection of the Church, "at-least-God-loves-me". Professionally, John Betjeman has always lived in fear of the poverty which he believes will eventually drive him to the workhouse door – has his passion for churches been an instinctive effort to protect himself, in this life and the next? Further, if you feel yourself to be egregious, eccentric, "an only child, deliciously misunderstood", the Church can cater comfortably for you. (His television broadcasts on churches often contained clergymen who were unusual in their hobbies or their gait or their demeanour.)

*   *   *

How long was the peril, how breathless the day,
In topaz and beryl, the sun dies away,
His rays lying static at quarter to six
On polychromatical lacing of bricks.
Good Lord, as the angelus floats down the road,
Byzantine St. Barnabas, be Thine Abode.

For "Low" and "High" in Betjeman country read "affection" and "reverence". Village churches, such as Speckleby in Lincolnshire, are friendly local characters, in homespun clothing; further up the scale St. Barnabas, Oxford, may not be approached so familiarly. Is this the only church in Britain established by a publisher? Thomas Combe, of the Clarendon Press at Oxford University nearby, worried that the young people in his employ might not have moral reference points, founded the church in time with the Oxford Movement. Therefore, St. Barnabas, Oxford, is certainly "High". The Byzantine suggestions continue right through the church, to the lustrous pulpit, the baldachin at the font, the soaring roof, to the little shrines in the corners. The sanctuary gilding exudes devotion, the four beasts of the Apocalypse patrol the high altar, commemorative plaques recall Rathbones and Ridgways.

In other churches "High" means "commanding": Christ Church in Swindon exercises its full peal of ten bells to call citizens to attention:

Oh brick-built breeding boxes of new souls,
Hear how the pealing through the louvres rolls!
Now birth and death-reminding bells ring clear,
Loud under 'planes and over changing gear.

And the environment echoes the peal – the headstones and the church foundations rise high above the cars in the car park.

*   *   *

In 1974 *The City of London Churches* by John Betjeman appeared – a slim, illustrated booklet with an introduction, several long descriptions and thirty-nine churches.

Their names read like a medieval, celestial team of hymn writers: St. Andrew-by-the-Wardrobe, St. Bartholomew-the-Great (and the-Less), St. Benet, Paul's Wharf, St. Botolph, Aldersgate (and Aldgate and Bishopsgate), St. Clement, Eastcheap, St. Dunstan-in-the-West, St. Ethelburga, Bishopsgate, St. Giles, Cripplegate – which is not what it sounds: this cripplegate, this cover'd walk, admitted Queen Elizabeth I on her

Christ Church, Swindon

accession to the throne and, five hundred years earlier, Edmond
the Martyr's body went in the opposite direction. St. Giles himself, though, was not the full physical shilling – was he the deer
who, pursued and shot in the leg by Charlemagne, suddenly
turned into a friar with an arrow in his leg? St. Giles always
walked with a crutch, thereafter – Charlemagne cannot have
been the same person either.

Betjeman's note in the *Parish Guide* is surprisingly terse –
"Oasis in Barbican. Double-aisled; large; early 16th century;
much restored. 17th century top stage to tower. Furnishings
from St. Luke, Old Street. Milton buried here." And suitably

commemorated in a small plaque in the centre aisle: "Near this spot was buried John Milton author of Paradise Lost; Born 1608 Died 1674."

Cromwell married in this transept, so did Sir Thomas More's parents. Betjeman's history, so personal in the village churches, comes to life from the school books in this vaulted, bright, clear, open church. In his descriptions of the other thirty-eight in the booklet, history and architecture merge with worship in the same statement which has characterised all his poetry of place – that we are our environment, we are part of its fabric and, our topography is part of our morality.

In recent years John Betjeman worshipped frequently in Holy Trinity, Sloane Street.

> The tall red house soars upward to the stars,
> The doors are chased with sardonyx and gold,
> And in the long white room
> Thin drapery draws backward to unfold
> Cadogan Square between the window-bars . . .

Enter through a clear glass door from Sloane Street, under the five fine stone arches. On the ceiling, the moulded bosses in vivid lime-green and red bear the Cadogan crest – the fifth earl founded the church. The east window, with forty-eight panels in procession, raises the eyes and the heart. Adam, Enoch, Abraham, Noah and the saints – including St. Patrick – stand four-square, side by side across the wall in muted stained glass. Angels in bronze, unfurling long narrow scrolls, flank the chancel.

On one wall, Elizabeth Laura Olliffe is recalled by her sisters, Florence Bell and Sophie Kitcat; pray too, for the souls of Mary Florence Octavia Chown, Florence Dorothea Fearnley-Whittingstaff, Flying Officer Tickle.

To the left of the high altar, beneath a baldachin, on an altar table bearing the words "All Men Seek Thee", the celebrant is concluding his blessing: "Go in Peace to Love and Serve the Lord".

Between twenty and thirty people bow their heads to receive it. Another small congregation, ghostly now, wafts to mind: St. Saviour's, Aberdeen Park, a few miles away, lies dark and silent.

In a poem called "Church of England thoughts occasioned by hearing the bells of Magdalen Tower from the Botanic Garden, Oxford, on St. Mary Magdalen's Day", John Betjeman made his bells universal, calling souls everywhere to *Matins*, or Eucharist, "in country churches old and pale", or in "chapels-of-ease by railway lines", or "churches blue with incense mist". Thus, too, with his worship. For Holy Trinity, Sloane Street, for "High", "Broad" or "Low" in Betjeman country, read St. Saviour's, Aberdeen Park.

> Wonder beyond Time's wonders, that Bread so white and small
> Veiled in golden curtains, too mighty for men to see,
> Is the Power which sends the shadows up this polychrome wall,
> Is God who created the present, the chain-smoking millions
> and me;
> Beyond the throb of the engines is the throbbing heart of all –
> Christ, at this Highbury altar, I offer myself to Thee.

CHAPTER
TWELVE
METRO-LAND

Gaily into Ruislip Gardens
    Runs the red electric train,
With a thousand Ta's and Pardon's
    Daintily alights Elaine;
Hurries down the concrete station
With a frown of concentration,
Out into the outskirt's edges
Where a few surviving hedges
Keep alive our lost Elysium – rural Middlesex again.

On a BBC television programme in 1973 John Betjeman was seen to walk from the bar of a typical small railway station, out on to the platform and board a train. The camera fastened upon a suggestion adorning the door, "Live in Metro-Land". On the sound track, when the music had abated gently, the poet's voice was heard saying, "When I was a boy 'Live in Metro-Land' was the slogan."

And hundreds of thousands of people did, in rows and rows of houses with stained-glass lights in the tall front doors, small gardens in front, enough for a rose bush or two, red tiles on the roof, perhaps a bay window, "Oakdene", "Ash Dell", "Willow Bank". Metro-Land was – and remains – a land of villas. "You paid a deposit," reminded the television screen, "and eventually we hope you had your own house with its garage and front garden and back garden – a verge in front of your house and grass and a tree for the dog."

Metro-Land was the domestic federation of those dormitory homelands in Middlesex and Buckinghamshire – Ruislip and Pinner and Harrow and Neasden and Wembley. Here was a significant social and sociological development – London man could realise his rural dream, even if it had been provided for him by a speculative builder. Metro-Land was created by the coming of the railways, by the almost mighty Metropolitan Railway which went forth, north and west, from Baker Street Station.

> Early Electric! With what radiant hope
>   Men formed this many-branched electrolier,
> Twisted the flex around the iron rope
>   And let the dazzling vacuum globes hang clear,
> And then with hearts the rich contrivance fill'd
> Of copper, beaten by the Bromsgrove Guild.

John Betjeman even wrote a hymn of praise to the buffet at

Baker Street Station. In the television programme he sat in its Chiltern Court Restaurant, wondering whether the wives from Pinner and Ruislip waited after a day's shopping, for their husbands to finish work "in Cheapside and Mincing Lane" and then go home together.

The restaurant took its name from Chiltern Court, the block of flats with which the station was topped in 1929. The original intention had been to erect a hotel or a cinema, but when H. G. Wells and Arnold Bennett came to live in Chiltern Court, its reputation – "the most elegant place in London to live" – was assured. The restaurant has been gutted, the doors are closed. Stuck to one of them, a note, written on brown paper: "Ann – hope you get to see this message, sorry about wrong directions. The Allsop Arms is on Gloucester Place remember. Hope to see you there later on. Bye for now and love Brian. X" The stained-glass frieze, with its doltish medieval figures, still lines the lintel; in the restoration, the decorative panels and the mock-medieval crests inside will vanish.

Early Electric! Sit you down and see,
    'Mid this fine woodwork and a smell of dinner,
A stained-glass windmill and a pot of tea,
    And sepia views of leafy lanes in PINNER–
Then visualize, far down the shining lines,
Your parents' homestead set in murmuring pines.

Smoothly from HARROW, passing PRESTON ROAD,
    They saw the last green fields and misty sky,
At NEASDEN watched a workmen's train unload,
    And, with the morning villas sliding by,
They felt so sure on their electric trip
That Youth and Progress were in partnership.

By the last years of the last century the Metropolitan Railway
Company actually owned vast acreages. Its trains ran through
many thousands more, but its directors wanted some greater
return on their money than mere train fares. Astutely they took
advantage of an earlier Act of Parliament which had permitted
it to issue building licences and sell ground rents on the lands
it owned in the City of London. As the century turned, the
Metropolitan decided to develop the fields by its lines in the
suburbs. The acres were quartered and sold off as sites – to individual purchasers or in blocks to speculative builders. After the
Great War, the Metropolitan Country Estates Company issued
advertising pamphlets extolling the joys of Metro-Land – the
name it had coined in 1915. They would build you a house
or a bungalow, to your own choice of design, for £200 down
and the balance paid quarterly at six per cent over fifteen years.
"Hearts are lighter, eyes are brighter, In Metro-Land, in Metro-
Land" sang George R. Sims, and Evelyn Waugh took the image
a little further in *Decline and Fall*, creating a character by name
of "Margot Metroland". The couple, therefore, in Betjeman's
poem, "The Metropolitan Railway", could have bought a house
in Ruislip or Wembley or Pinner for £350 (a three-bedroom
villa) or £425 (a four-bedroom residence).

Early Electric! Maybe even here
    They met that evening at six-fifteen
Beneath the hearts of this electrolier
    And caught the first non-stop to WILLESDEN GREEN,
Then out and on, through rural RAYNER'S LANE
To autumn-scented Middlesex again.

Willesden was a less salubrious forerunner of the type of housing development which became Metro-Land: smaller, meaner,

FOR COUNTRY WALKS

HARROW WEALD
BY THROUGH BAKERLOO TRAINS
TO PINNER AND HATCH END

Sᵀ ALBANS
BY MOTOR BUS ROUTE 84
DAILY FROM GOLDERS GREEN

DENHAM BY TRAM FROM
SHEPHERDS BUSH ᴼᴿ HAMMERSMITH
OR BY DISTRICT RAILWAY DIRECT

UNDERGROUND

THE OP

grey or yellow bricks, clumsy bay windows, low walls shod with ornamented cast iron, a smattering of tiles in the sheltered area before the front door, feeble stained glass. Willesden wanders on and on from the Underground, a depressing, bustling thorough-fare of small shops and large pubs. Now and again, a rococo cornice, some craftsman's outburst of whim, perches on the roof-ridge of a red-brick shop: merchandise overflows through the doors, ladders, chairs, mattresses, pets. All colours, all accents, pubs with high nicotine-stained ceilings, dados running around from saloon to public bar; walk on through Willesden, turn its long corners, past the industrial estates, past the hulks of old cars, piles of rubbish, oil drums, beer cans, old newspapers that despoil "open" ground behind high wire fences. This is a desert, a wasteland, an environmental scab. But ahead, an oasis of green and stone, on the apex of Neasden Lane, a church, and, more absorbingly, a churchyard.

> Come walk with me, my love, to Neasden Lane.
> The chemicals from various factories
> Have bitten deep into the Portland stone
> And streaked the white Carrara of the graves
> Of many a Pooter and his Caroline,
> Long laid to rest among these dripping trees;

Unless you were seeking Betjeman country you would not, in such unprepossessing terrain, seek out Willesden church-yard. The church is locked and barred, some of the monuments in the churchyard are damaged.

And this, my love, is Laura Seymour's grave –
"So long the loyal counsellor and friend"
Of that Charles Reade whose coffin lies with hers.
Was she his mistress?

The inscriptions read ". . . a brilliant artist, a humble Christian, a charitable woman, a loving daughter, sister and friend who lived for others from her childhood . . . When the eye saw her, it blessed her, for her face was sunshine her voice was melody . . ." and she died on September the 27th, 1879, at the age of 59 years.

The sun would send
Last golden streaks of mild October light
On tarred and weather-boarded barn and shed.
Blue bonfire smoke would hang among the trees;
And in the little stucco hermitage
Did Laura gently stroke her lover's head?

She was an actress, he was a playwright, their relationship was said to be platonic. He was a scholar and a barrister too, with an advanced sense of social justice, who made no money from the theatre, wrote successful novels, among them *The Cloister and the Hearth*.

And did her Charles look up into her eyes
For loyal counsel there? I do not know.
Doubtless some pedant for his Ph.D.
Has ascertained the facts, or I myself
Might find them in the public libraries.

Elsewhere in the churchyard at Willesden lie Bakers and Finches and Postlethwaites. Snapped-off columns take on a new, van-dalised symbolism here. So walk on – the wilderness awaits you. Across the road and down a little from Willesden churchyard stands a huge white oblong palace, clad in snowy stone and glass, acres of glass, window after window after window, rectangles that shine in the sun. Out of place in this countryside, environmentally but not sociologically, this is Chancel House where the citizens queue for the dole; but – it is called the Department of *Em*ployment?

Neasden Station squats on the crest of a hill. Behind it stretch long wide acres of railway lands; in the distance the turrets of Wembley Stadium. The climb from the station is steep; the shops at the summit, in Neasden Parade, contribute the added attractions of the brochure, built to serve these new garden suburbs.

A younger, brighter, homelier Metro-Land:
"Rusholme", "Rustles", "Rustlings", "Rusty Tiles",
"Rose Hatch", "Rose Hill", "Rose Lea", "Rose Mount",
"Rose Roof",
Each one is slightly different from the next,
A bastion of individual taste
On fields that once were bright with buttercups.

This is Wembley, next village to Neasden, home of the stadium, and gaunt in front of it, empty Hitlerian palaces, a runaway, forgotten Nuremberg of former imperial celebrations, ghosts of the Empire Exhibition of the twenties.

On Oakington Avenue no more "Rusholme", "Rustles" or "Rustlings" – only numbers, the new egalitarian snobbery, or a lingering "St. Denys" or "Heliopolis".

When melancholy Autumn comes to Wembley
And electric trains are lighted after tea
The poplars near the Stadium are trembly
With their tap and tap and whispering to me,
Like the sound of little breakers
Spreading out along the surf-line
When the estuary's filling
With the sea.

*   *   *

In moments of spiritual fantasy – and with, perhaps, more than mere whimsy – John Betjeman wished to be considered a Harrovian rather than a Marlburian. Handing out assorted collected school boaters in party humour he always chose the Harrow ribbon: around the piano he led with the Harrow School Song. The fantasy carried over into his poetry:

Then Harrow-on-the-Hill's a rocky island
And Harrow churchyard full of sailors' graves
And the constant click and kissing of the trolley buses hissing
Is the level to the Wealdstone turned to waves
And the rumble of the railway
Is the thunder of the rollers
As they gather up for plunging
Into caves.

Beyond Harrow, stretching north, make a worthwhile Betjemanesque diversion. Grim's Dyke, now a hotel, was designed
by Betjeman's hero, Norman Shaw: on television the poet of
Metro-Land said he always regarded Grim's Dyke "as the proto-
type of all houses in southern England". This is the house where
William Schwenck Gilbert lived and died. "Sir William
loved Grim's Dyke" says the hotel brochure, "and lavished
much care on the house and gardens. His Music Room, now
called the Iolanthe Hall, stands perhaps as his best memorial
at Grim's Dyke, with its Minstrel Gallery, Barrel Ceiling and
magnificent Cornish Alabaster Fireplace, a copy from his London home in Harrington Gardens which Sir William admired
so much . . . Visitors can stroll down to the lake, where sadly
Sir William died. It was while he was teaching two young ladies
to swim that one got out of her depth and called for help. Sir

William gallantly plunged in to save her but the sudden exertion proved too much for his heart and he died that evening." Tall chimneys, Tudor gables, leaded panes; the lawns are still impeccable, the rhododendrons wonderfully profuse, the box and privet glowing and neat, the lake is overgrown. Visitors – the Harrow East Conservative Association, Tridac Dental Equipment, Aro Plastics – may commemorate Sir William, if they wish, in "the unique Gilbert and Sullivan Sunday Soirees".

> Funereal from Harrow draws the train,
> On, on, northwestwards, London far away,
> And stations start to look quite countrified.
> Pinner, a parish of a thousand souls,
> Til the railways gave it many thousands more.

Pinner is famous for its village Fair
Where once a year, St. John the Baptist's Day,
Shows all the climbing High Street filled with stalls.
It is the Feast Day of the Parish Saint,
A mediaeval Fair in Metro-Land.

Is there no end to these landscapes? On and on and on –
Rayner's Lane, Northwood, Moor Park, Rickmansworth, to
the depths of Chorleywood, in whose brochure John Betjeman
took such a delight: "It's the trees, the fairy dingles and a
hundred and one things in which Dame Nature's fingers have
lingered long in setting out this beautiful array of trout stream,
wooded slope, meadow and hill-top sites. Send a postcard for
the homestead of your dreams, to Loudwater Estate,
Chorleywood."

Metro-Land lives: the Volvo rampages, men in shorts on
sunny days trim their hedges with electric caution. But few of
the original Metro-Land front doors survive with their small
ovals of stained glass, the chrome knocker just beneath. They
have been porched, panelled, painted in brighter colours.

Metro-Land's appeal for Betjeman lay in its railway heritage.
In a talk on the BBC Home Service on Sunday the 10th of March,
1940 he began, "This is an odd thing to ask you to do on a
fine Sunday morning, but I want you to imagine yourself in the
waiting room of a railway station on a wet evening . . ." And
he went on to describe the room in all the details of its railway
trappings. ". . . the black horse-hair benches and chairs, the
mahogany table, the grate with its winking fire, the large framed
photographs of yellowing views of crowded esplanades and ivy-
mantled ruins, the framed advertisement for the company's
hotel at Strathmacgregor, electric light, exquisite cuisine, lifts
to all floors, within five minutes of sea and pier; the gaslight
roaring a friendly buzz of conversation of other people also
awaiting trains . . ." Elsewhere, he swore an ambition to retire
from all poetry and journalism and become the station-master
at Ongar on the Underground's Central Line.

Metro-Land is quintessential Betjeman country. Trains stop
at quite small stations, high flights of steps out into innocuous
lobbies, one ticket desk, a collector's cubicle, then the suburban
road. As far as eye can see, rows and rows of houses, bow-
fronted, red-tiled, timber-striped. "Cottage at Prestwood",
"Near Great Missenden", "Haydon Hall, Eastcote", "At Icken-
ham" – the brochures, wrote John Betjeman, "tempted the Lon-
doner out on to new estates, far beyond the Wembley
Exhibition."

METRO-LAND

PRICE TWO-PENCE

And the developers kept the dreams of taste alive. "Although the Company aims at introducing all classes into the community, it is not intended to indiscriminately mix all classes and sizes of houses together; different portions of the estate lend themselves to different types and sizes of houses. Thus one of the neat village houses which are being erected near Ruislip Station would be completely lost amid the wooded heights of Northwood, which demand more stately architecture, with its more massive setting." But today, the red electric train suffers less opulent architecture at Ruislip Gardens. Slabs of concrete, striped in brick, nearby blocks of plain flats, Elaine's rural idyll is less ideal.

Well cut Windsmoor flapping lightly,
    Jacqmar scarf of mauve and green
Hiding hair which, Friday nightly,
    Delicately drowns in Drene;
Fair Elaine the bobby-soxer,
Fresh-complexioned with Innoxa,
Gains the garden – father's hobby –
Hangs her Windsmoor in the lobby,
Settles down to sandwich supper and the television screen.

Betjeman's Elaine is an emblem. "I was walking down a High
Road in the gallant County of Middlesex on a hot Saturday
morning," he wrote in 1960. "Black glass fascias of chain stores,
each at a different height from its neighbour, looked like a row
of shiny goloshes on the feet of buildings. Corner shops and
supermarkets seemed to be covered in coloured plastic, like the
goods they sold. All too soon the wrappings would be torn off
and left to blow about municipal rose beds and recreation
grounds. Somewhere, if I dared to raise my eyes above my head,
there must have been sky."

From the island platform of Ruislip Gardens you can still
see sky, and, over these seas of red tiles, over the low ridges
of the factories and warehouses, the spire of Harrow, the distant
shores of Metro-Land . . .

Gentle Brent, I used to know you
    Wandering Wembley-wards at will,
Now what change your waters show you
    In the meadowlands you fill!
Recollect the elm-trees misty
And the footpaths climbing twisty
Under cedar-shaded palings,
Low laburnum-leaned-on railings,
Out of Northolt on and upward to the heights of Harrow Hill.

POSTSCRIPT

Betjeman country is not, has never been, despite his sense of humour, and the affection in which he is held, a place composed entirely of calm and light. At the end of the road two impressions remain, one vital, one delightful. First of all, John Betjeman is misperceived – and probably always has been. A reluctance to offend people face-to-face is misconstrued as pusillanimity: his sense of rhyme is often misinterpreted as an easy option. The cuddly and amusing image persists – to his own intellectual detriment. But the teddy-bear poet, whose work achieves deep, deep popular penetration across all social and educational strata, is more accurately the reporter-poet, the observer-poet, the misanthrope-poet; for too long now his verses have been dismissed by critics simply because he appeared to present an amiable face to the world.

In the Introduction to *Slick But Not Streamlined*, a small anthology of Betjeman's poetry and prose chosen specially for the American market in 1974, W. H. Auden wrote, "I am tempted at this point to try to forestall any idiotic critic who may think – whether with approval or disapproval is all one, for both are equally wrongheaded – that Mr. Betjeman's poems are trivial, that because he does not write earnestly about religion, love, and death, he is lacking in real faith and sincere emotion, but I realise that the blind cannot be argued into vision." The key word there is "earnestly", and it is a word which does not easily apply to John Betjeman – especially when he combines his love of buildings with his fear for what the bureaucrats and the politicians are doing to our environment.

> I have a Vision of The Future, chum,
>   The workers' flats in fields of soya beans
>   Tower up like silver pencils, score on score:
>   And Surging Millions hear the Challenge come
>   From microphones in communal canteens
>   "No Right! No Wrong! All's perfect, evermore."

Further on in *Slick But Not Streamlined*, the poet himself discussed his own passion for topographical verse. "Until the middle of the nineteenth century poets who wrote in the visual manner confined themselves for the most part to descriptions of nature. This was because natural scenery was more in evidence than it is now. The tradition has died hard and it is still thought by some people that all visual poetry should mention stooks and wains and elderberry bushes." And in the conclusion, beside his much-quoted love of Pont Street, and gas-light and suburbs and churches and railways, he was emphatic: "They are, many of them, part of my background. From them I try to create an atmosphere which will be remembered by those who have had a similar background, when England is all council houses and trunk roads and steel and glass factory blocks in the New Europe of after the War."

But he never, anywhere, argued that such topography as he wished to immortalise had to be written about in hushed or ponderous tones, that reverence had to be stirred up.

> Come, friendly bombs, and fall on Slough
> It isn't fit for humans now,
> There isn't grass to graze a cow
> Swarm over, Death!

The misanthropy and the struggle to preserve the old values collide with a crash, and those who complained that Betjeman always lacked the final drop of acid which marks the true satirist cannot have read the poem too closely.

> Mess up the mess they call a town –
> A house for ninety-seven down
> And once a week a half-a-crown
> For twenty years,

> And get that man with double chin
> Who'll always cheat and always win,
> Who washes his repulsive skin
> In women's tears,

> And smash his desk of polished oak
> And smash his hands so used to stroke
> And stop his boring dirty joke
> And make him yell.

Did he walk through Slough – he was only in his twenties then – gritting his teeth at the developers and wishing that his physical stature was great, greater, greatest, that he could reach down and smash this appalling life which speculators and profiteers were foisting upon us?

> In labour-saving homes, with care
> Their wives frizz out peroxide hair
> And dry it in synthetic air
> And paint their nails.

Arrive in Slough on a dim afternoon, see the rows and rows of utter factories with occasional houses flecked through them – the weeds have overtaken the few old flowers.

*   *   *

The second, and more rewarding, concession of travelling on a Betjeman ticket is gained from the power of his observation. In all the journeys he himself has made in the past sixty years or so, since he began to explore London as a schoolboy, he has epitomised the old advice to tourists and travelling schoolchildren – "Look up." Further, what Auden said of Goethe's self-revelations in his *Italian Journey* applies to John Betjeman too, especially architecturally. "He always refused to separate the beautiful from the necessary for he was convinced that one cannot really appreciate the beauty of anything without understanding what made it possible and why it came into being." Stand, then, in a small country church, put aside for the moment Betjeman's exclusive attachment to only the Highest of the High, and the edifice and its restorer come to life, for better or for worse, under his scrutiny.

> Of marble brown and veinéd
> He did the pulpit make;
> He order'd windows stainéd
> Light red and crimson lake.
> Sing on, with hymns uproarious,
> Ye humble and aloof,
> Look up! and oh how glorious
> He has restored the roof!

In every parish church there is a distinct feeling that John Betjeman has been, and approved, a sort of enquiring but benign "Kilroy was here". And overall there is the distinct impression that he really prefers buildings, loves them more than he loves mankind, sees them as symbol and metaphor all in one: most crucially of all he can never distinguish the building from its occupants or users. The buildings become the people who are attached to them – indeed, he regrets, or so it would seem, that the people do not more often take on the characteristics of the buildings, rather than the other way around.

> And where's the roof of golden thatch?
> The chimney-stack of stone?
> The crown-glass panes that used to match
> Each sunset with their own?

Oh now the walls are red and smart,
The roof has emerald tiles.
The neon sign's a work of art
And visible for miles.

*   *   *

With some justification it may be argued that John Betjeman has not been a poetic innovator in terms of form. Indeed, he even confessed to having taken many of his metres from poets of previous centuries whose work he has admired. Argue, too, that he should have made the most of his liking for brand names, place names, eccentric personal names and might have turned to advantage these fresh sounds, developed this language new to poetry: instead he was content to use sounds only for rhymes. But against that, by using such familiar and domestic terminology he became perhaps the only poet in this century to reach all levels of intellect, across all strata of birth and education – and he had begun to do so before radio and television had brought him to a mass audience.

His humanity becomes most apparent when you are confronted with a place which he described vividly, but which to a traveller is impenetrable. The area known as North Oxford, now melded into the rest of the city, is a land which keeps strangers at a distance. Betjeman, with a couple of strokes of his pen – in prose curiously, a medium which he has always considered inferior to poetry – laid it bare. "The inner North Oxford is a life in itself," he wrote in *An Oxford University Chest*, "a home of married dons, dons' widows, retired clergymen, retired dons, preparatory schools, theological seminaries, bicycle sheds, ladies' colleges, tea-parties, perambulators and peace except where the Banbury and Woodstock roads roar past the diversity of their buildings."

To my foreign eye North Oxford is a land of leafy drives, sober, not to say sombre, houses, formidable front doors, an excess of politeness, angular, slow-moving figures walking for ever along the pavements, the flash of a young wife behind the steering-wheel of the smaller Volvo, children addressing each other loftily from the saddles of expensive bicycles as they wheel round and round, sure of their future lives, the mica-glints of stained glass in the weak spring sunlight, and an acquired silence.

I have taken lessons, though, from the poet, whose early explorations of North Oxford amounted almost to anthropology. He offers "three formulae for the observant in North Oxford by the use of which they may tell who lives in which house, regardless of the style in which it is built".

(1) A bicycle shed in the garden and a bright red brick appendage in the Tudor style with stained glass; a large house and an ill-kept garden mean a Theological College or something to do with a school.

(2) Lace curtains in the window, well-kept garden, no bicycle shed, all the windows shut, gas-light, means a retired clergyman or clergyman's widow.

(3) Dark blue or orange curtains or no curtains at all. A bare table except for a bowl of hyacinths in the ground floor window; all the windows open; tooth-brushes airing on the bathroom window ledge; a bicycle shed for three bicycles; an old Morris outside – all means a don's house and probably one who takes in senior students as lodgers during term time.

*   *   *

In some ways the best journeys of all in Betjeman country are those which still have to be taken. "Dear Mary", he wrote to Lady Wilson,

> Yes, it will be bliss
> To go with you by train to Diss,
> Your walking shoes upon your feet;
> We'll meet, my sweet, at Liverpool Street.

And when I get there, as in time I shall, because the journey goes on, what shall I find? In Pontefract will there be licorice fields and will there be a girl?

> Red hair she had and golden skin,
> Her sulky lips were shaped for sin,
> Her sturdy legs were flannel-slack'd,
> The strongest legs in Pontefract.

Or perhaps a night-club, in a row of shops whose living quarters overhead are half-timbered in a town like St. Albans, and a lady in pensioned rouge sits by the bar recalling better days.

> When Boris used to call in his Sedanca,
> When Teddy took me down to his estate
> When my nose excited passion,
> When my clothes were in the fashion,
> When my beaux were never cross if I was late

In Betjeman country I finally found that the reality was not so important. I trudged for hours, in search of "the Cottage of the Aged" near Waterloo: then he told me that it never existed, "only in Dickens". Nothing happened in Speckleby, either, in the county of Lincs.: that was all a wild fiction to fit some euphonious place name. This does not affect the belief. When I return to Southend it will not be crowded this time, no hordes of red faces above pale bodies and ice-cream, it will again be a serene architectural gem of white clapboard and wrought iron and respectable terraces.

It occurs to me now that in my travels I may have unduly emphasised the gloominess of some parts of Betjeman country. The City of London is deeply depressing, an uncaring place, except for its magic on a Sunday morning, when the clink of coins being counted is no longer audible. Metro-Land, especially the acres around Willesden and Neasden, may once have been beautiful: today it is an endurance test for the eyes, although when John Betjeman saw it first it was London's brave new world. Even Cornwall, so beloved that his granddaughter is called Endellion after a favourite parish saint, contains intimatations of his mortality, moods that are deep and still and frightening.

He may be the only poet who has ever ranged so comprehensively across the family budget – who else immortalised "Banana Blush" and railways and small churches and Woolworths and the Co-op and the Regent Palace? He is certain now to be the last. The places he described have disappeared into the memories of those who knew Betjeman country between the softness of the twenties and thirties, and the excitement of the sixties. But there is another reason. Whatever his critics have said, anybody who tries to emulate John Betjeman's style is immediately recognised in the effort, and dismissed as not being original. Similarly there is no other place quite like Betjeman country. Whether it ever really existed outside his poems – and how dangerous it is to generalise about "the poet of the particular" – is irrelevant.

BIBLIOGRAPHY

E ven though the literature *by* John Betjeman is, one way and another, substantial, the literature *about* him is surprisingly slim. The most outstanding short source is a pamphlet entitled *John Betjeman* by John Press, edited by Ian Scott-Kilvert and published for the British Council by the Longman Group, London, 1974. Otherwise this bibliography does not list all the various speeches, talks, broadcasts and other material, newspaper and magazine articles, and critical surveys either written by the Poet Laureate or discussing him, nor does it include the many anthologies to which he has contributed prefaces or introductions.

BY JOHN BETJEMAN

Mount Zion, London, 1931, private publication.
Ghastly Good Taste, London, 1933, Chapman & Hall; re-issued London, 1970, Anthony Blond.
Cornwall: A Shell Guide, 1934, London, Faber & Faber, and subsequently revised.
Devon: A Shell Guide, London, 1936, the Architectural Press.
Continual Dew, London, 1937, John Murray.
An Oxford University Chest, London, 1938, John Miles.
Old Lights for New Chancels, London, 1940, John Murray.
New Bats in Old Belfries, London, 1945, John Murray.
Slick But Not Streamlined, New York, 1947, Doubleday.
Murray's Buckinghamshire Architectural Guide, London, 1948, John Murray.
Selected Poems, London, 1948, John Murray.
Murray's Berkshire Architectural Guide, London, 1949, John Murray.
First and Last Loves, London, 1952, John Murray.
Poems in the Porch, London, 1955, S.P.C.K.
A Few Late Chrysanthemums, London, 1954, John Murray.
Collins Guide to Parish Churches of England and Wales Including Isle of Man (Ed.), London, 1958, Collins.
Summoned by Bells, London, 1960, John Murray.
High & Low, London, 1966, John Murray.
Victorian and Edwardian London from Old Photographs, London, 1969, Batsford.
A Pictorial History of English Architecture, London, 1970, John Murray.
The City of London Churches, London, 1974, Pitkin Pictorials, Ltd.

Victorian and Edwardian Oxford from Old Photographs, London, 1971, Batsford.
London's Historic Railway Stations, London, 1972, John Murray.
A Nip in the Air, London, 1974, John Murray.
Uncollected Poems, London, 1982, John Murray.
And – above all – *The Collected Poems of John Betjeman*, first published London, 1958, John Murray, and subsequently revised.

ALSO CONSULTED

Amory, Mark (Ed.) – *The Letters of Evelyn Waugh*, London, 1980, Weidenfeld and Nicolson.
Davie, Michael (Ed.) – *The Diaries of Evelyn Waugh*, London, 1976, Weidenfeld and Nicolson.
MacNeice, Louis – *The Strings are False*, London, 1965, Faber & Faber.
Stanford, Derek – *John Betjeman: A Study*, London, 1961, Neville Spearman.
Taylor-Martin, Patrick – *John Betjeman, His Life and Work*, London, 1983, Allen Lane.

TOPOGRAPHICAL

Of the wide range of topographical books which proved useful, including parish magazines, local leaflets, county publications, the most lasting books seemed the most sensible to mention.

London: The Northern Reaches, by Robert Colville, London, 1951, Robert Hale.
Hampstead and Highgate in Old Photographs, 1870–1918, by Christina M. Gee, London, 1974, High Hill Press.
The Companion Guide to London, by David Piper, London, 1964, Collins.
Dictionary of City of London Street Names, by Al Smith, Newton Abbot, 1970, David & Charles.
Semi-Detached London, by Alan A. Jackson, London, 1973, Allen & Unwin.
A History of London Transport, Vols. I & II, by T. C. Barker & Michael Robbins, London, 1963 and 1974, Allen & Unwin.
Oxford, by James Morris, London, 1965, Faber & Faber.
The Oxford Book of Oxford, chosen and edited by Jan Morris, 1978, Oxford University Press.

ACKNOWLEDGMENTS

The author wishes to make grateful acknowledgment to the following:
Sir John Betjeman, for his unstinting permission to quote so extensively from his works; and for his time and information; his secretary, Elizabeth Moore, for her assistance in tracing sources; Mrs. Leonora Ison, for her enthusiasm as well as her efficiency, and her husband, Walter Ison, who contributed his time and his knowledge so unselfishly; James Ravilious, for his commitment to the task; Mrs. Gwynned Gosling, Librarian, Highgate Literary and Scientific Institution, for her assistance in tracing early textual and pictorial material, to the Director and Staff of the London Library for their customary tirelessness; the Headmaster and Librarian at Marlborough, and especially a Master there, Michael Justin Davies, for extending the hospitality of the school and its archives; the President and Bursar of Magdalen College, Oxford, and the parish of St. Minver, Cornwall, for permission to photograph their buildings and environs; the Director and Staff of the National Library of Ireland, Kildare Street, Dublin, for assistance rendered and for permission to reproduce photographs from the Lawrence Collection, and the Staff of the County Library of Westmeath at Mullingar for contributing material on Sir John Piers.

Publications such as the *Daily Telegraph, The Times, The Spectator, The Times Literary Supplement,* were always made available to me, as were the archives of the BBC, and I am especially grateful to Edward Mirzoeff, producer of such Betjeman television classics as *Metro-Land* and *A Passion for Churches,* for his valuable suggestions and directions; likewise Lord Horder who supplied me with some Betjeman poems set to music and Sue Freathy and Michael Shaw at Curtis Brown Ltd., who were both practical and enthusiastic in their assistance.

Acknowledgments are especially due to my secretary, Sheila Jordan, for searching innumerable archives so diligently, and for her constant supportiveness; to Tracy Loveman, for impeccable and expeditious typing, to Amanda Batten and Mary-Lou Nesbitt for attention to detail, to Sharyn Troughton who designed this book, and to Mr. Jock Murray at John Murray

Ltd. for his guidance and for supplying material in a generous fashion. And I wish to thank particularly Ion Trewin for editorial attention of rare unselfishness, his family for their endless patience and hospitality – and Brigid Roden, yet again.

Thanks are also due to the following individuals and institutions for allowing us to use the following material from their archives, and for their help in locating it. Page 22, Highgate West Hill, circa 1904: London Borough of Camden. Pages 26–7, Byron House School photograph: Highgate Literary and Scientific Institution. Pages 33, 36–7, Port Isaac, circa 1906, and pages 44–5, Chapel Stile, Padstow: Royal Institution of Cornwall. Page 47, The Memorial Hall, Marlborough College: Collection of E. G. H. Kempson. Pages 66–7, Magdalen College from the bridge, circa 1924, and page 73, Oxford High Street, 192?: Central Library, Oxford.

Pages 106–7, Camden Town, circa 1904: London Borough of Camden. Pages 132–3, Tunbridge Wells Central Station, 193?: Tunbridge Wells County Library. Pages 146–7, Westgate, 1935, and pages 148–9, Westbrook, 1938: Central Library, Margate. Page 167, Hotwells, Bristol, and page 177, The Paragon, Bristol: Reece Winstone. Pages 174–5, Royal Crescent, Bath: Bath & Avon County Library.

Page 197, Christ Church, Swindon: Wiltshire County Council Library & Museum service. Pages 198–9, St. Giles Cripplegate, circa 1937: Guildhall Library. Original Metro-Land and London Transport posters on pages 201, 209 and 210-11, and the fifties photograph of the ticket hall of Baker Street Station on pages 204–5: London Transport Executive. The original Metro-Land housing advertisement on page 203, and the Metro-Land poster on page 219: Collection of D. F. Edwards. Pages 216–17, Pinner High Street in 1934, and the front cover, Pinner High Street at Fair Time, 1934: Harrow Civic Centre Library.

INDEX

231

A NIP IN THE AIR · London's Historic Railway S
Slick BUT NOT Streamlined · THE CITY OF LONDO
GHASTLY GOOD TASTE · Victor
PARISH CHURCHES of England & Wales · JOHN
CONTINUAL DEW · UNCOLLECTED POEMS · An
A FEW LATE CHRYSANTHEMUMS · OL
AND LOW · Murray's Buckinghamshire
A NIP IN THE AIR · London's Historic Railway S
Slick BUT NOT Streamlined · THE CITY OF LONDON
GHASTLY GOOD TASTE · Victor
PARISH CHURCHES of England & Wales · JOHN
CONTINUAL DEW · UNCOLLECTED POEMS · An
A FEW LATE CHRYSANTHEMUMS · OLI
AND LOW · Murray's Buckinghamshire
A NIP IN THE AIR · London's Historic Railway St
Slick BUT NOT Streamlined · THE CITY OF LONDON
PARISH CHURCHES of England & Wales · JOHN B
CONTINUAL DEW · UNCOLLECTED POEMS · An
A FEW LATE CHRYSANTHEMUMS · OLI
AND LOW · Murray's Buckinghamshire
A NIP IN THE AIR · London's Historic Railway St
Slick BUT NOT Streamlined · THE CITY OF LONDON
GHASTLY GOOD TASTE · Victoria
PARISH CHURCHES of England & Wales · JOHN B
CONTINUAL DEW · UNCOLLECTED POEMS · An
A FEW LATE CHRYSANTHEMUMS · OLD
AND LOW · Murray's Buckinghamshire G
A NIP IN THE AIR · London's Historic Railway Sta
Slick BUT NOT Streamlined · THE CITY OF LONDON
GHASTLY GOOD TASTE · Victoria
PARISH CHURCHES of England & Wales · JOHN B.
A FEW LATE CHRYSANTHEMUMS · OLD
AND LOW · Murray's Buckinghamshire G